The MYTH *of* GOOD CHRISTIAN PARENTING

HOW FALSE PROMISES BETRAYED A GENERATION OF EVANGELICAL FAMILIES

MARISSA FRANKS BURT *and*
KELSEY KRAMER McGINNIS

BrazosPress
a division of Baker Publishing Group
Grand Rapids, Michigan

Published by Brazos Press
a division of Baker Publishing Group
Grand Rapids, Michigan
BrazosPress.com

Printed in the United States of America

Library of Congress Cataloging-in-Publication Data
Names: Burt, Marissa, author | McGinnis, Kelsey Kramer, author
Title: The myth of good Christian parenting : how false promises betrayed a generation of evangelical families / Marissa Franks Burt and Kelsey Kramer McGinnis.
Description: Grand Rapids, Michigan : Brazos Press, a division of Baker Publishing Group, [2025] | Includes bibliographical references.
Identifiers: LCCN 2025015139 | ISBN 9781587436642 paperback | ISBN 9781493452118 ebook
Subjects: LCSH: Parenting—Religious aspects—Christianity | Child rearing—Religious aspects—Christianity
Classification: LCC BV4529 .B879 2025 | DDC 248.8/45—dc23/eng/20250530
LC record available at https://lccn.loc.gov/2025015139

Some names and details have been changed to protect the privacy of the individuals involved.

Cover design by Laura Powell

The authors are represented by WordServe Literary Group, www.wordserveliterary.com.

Baker Publishing Group publications use paper produced from sustainable forestry practices and postconsumer waste whenever possible.

25 26 27 28 29 30 31 7 6 5 4 3 2 1

"Through fascinating historical and theological exploration, Burt and McGinnis graciously identify the pitfalls of Christian parenting tropes and invite readers to a more holistic, grace-filled posture. As a remarried widow in a blended family of nine, I needed this reminder and encouragement that there is no 'one right way' to parent!"

—**Clarissa Moll**, four-time author and producer of *Christianity Today*'s *The Bulletin* podcast

"Christian parenting needs rescuing, and *The Myth of Good Christian Parenting* reveals where things went so far off track."

—**Sheila Wray Gregoire**, author of *The Great Sex Rescue* and founder of Bare Marriage

"Accessible and easy to understand, *The Myth of Good Christian Parenting* expertly surveys both the history of the evangelical parenting empire as well as the heartbreaking real-life stories from the children who survived it. Burt and McGinnis have created a groundbreaking and prophetic resource that will challenge and empower parents and other adults to see God's image reflected in children."

—**R. L. Stollar**, author of *The Kingdom of Children: A Liberation Theology*

"*The Myth of Good Christian Parenting* is a comprehensive reckoning of how abuse became sanctioned by Christian leadership. Religious trauma survivors know the fruit of that instruction all too well. This book belongs in every church, Christian counseling center, and trauma-informed therapist's office as a map that details how we got there and how we move forward differently."

—**Tia Levings**, author of the *New York Times* bestseller *A Well-Trained Wife* and *The Soul of Healing*

"*The Myth of Good Christian Parenting* offers a courageous and compassionate critique of popular evangelical parenting models that shaped generations. By examining the sociopolitical undercurrents and doctrinal shallowness that have often characterized so-called biblical parenting, this work challenges long-held assumptions with clarity and care. Rather than offering a new formula, it invites readers to reclaim agency, embrace curiosity, and move forward with wisdom and humility as they disentangle cultural norms from the heart of Scripture."

—**David and Amanda Erickson**, authors of *The Flourishing Family: A Jesus-Centered Guide to Parenting with Peace and Purpose* and founders of Flourishing Homes & Families

For my parents: my first teachers,
now two of my best friends
K. K. M.

For the children, whatever their age,
who have known domestic violence
M. F. B.

CONTENTS

PREFACE

In the spring of 2023, a friend posted a provocative question: What extremely niche topic would you write a book on if you had the time? I (Marissa) took a deep breath and shared an idea that had been simmering: a book that examined the history and theological assumptions behind "biblical" family-life teaching, including the resulting impact. I had been witnessing #ChurchToo and unaccountable church leaders in my own denomination, something that reminded me how certain theological frameworks could enable abuse. During this time, I was also drafting a novel that attempted to show the impact of high-control religious teachings. I recognized parallels between the ways churches were responding (or not) to criticisms leveled by survivors and accounts of how evangelicals were navigating inauthentic connection and estrangement within their immediate and extended families. I knew family-life teaching was an ecumenical touchpoint across denominations, and I wondered how it had shaped long-term relationships. It was difficult to sum up the concept in a brief reply to this friend's prompt, but the response was immediate.

"I think we need this." "I would read that in a heartbeat." "If it does not already exist, it really ought to be written!" "Wow. Please do that, though." These early ripples in my small social-media pond turned into the waves of people we would hear from over our months working on this project.

I (Kelsey) started researching for this book in 2018—sort of. My first baby was born in 2017, and when she was about one year old, I found myself wondering what I believed about some big things: human nature, sin, authority, autonomy, and my duties as a parent to my child and to God. Someone had given me a copy of Tedd Tripp's *Shepherding a Child's Heart* (1995), and as I read it, I felt confused and a little disturbed. I was in graduate school and working at a human rights research center that prioritized child advocacy through their work on child labor. I was used to speaking of children in terms of their rights, protection, and vulnerability in the world. Since I had grown up evangelical, Tripp's discussions of sin nature, corporal punishment, and parental authority were familiar, but the thought of applying them in my relationship with my daughter sent me into a spiral.

I ordered books, listened to podcasts, and followed influencers who taught about gentle parenting, attachment science, child development, positive discipline, and—of course—Christian parenting. What I found was a tribal, jagged landscape of conflicting advice and strong opinions. So I started a side project: researching the development of popular Christian parenting teaching, particularly related to beliefs about sin nature.

When I saw Marissa's post on social media, I immediately drafted a message saying that I had done some research and would be happy to share it if she thought it sounded helpful. Then I got cold feet and let the message sit in my drafts for a few days. After all, I thought, *I'm not a theologian. Maybe I'm not the right person to chime in here*. But I couldn't let it go. I sent it.

Together, we decided to take our study further. We set out to read primary sources, trace how different ideas developed, identify patterns across them, and consider the dynamics of American evangelicalism, which is itself a complicated subject to write about.[1] We wanted to offer a careful theological analysis and historical survey in order to help those touched by these resources examine the impact. We don't aim to speak authoritatively about every individual's experience, especially since it's impossible to state with certainty to what extent families adopted these ideas in practice. Our goal isn't to take down any particular figure or to suggest that there was nothing of merit in any of these resources. That said, we do think it is high time to hold the teachers, pastors, writers, influencers, and self-platformed Christian parenting "experts" accountable for propagating some sweeping myths about parenthood (and, in some cases, about Christian faith itself). We also hope this book offers access points for readers to understand their own experiences and formation.

We wanted to hear directly from people who were impacted by the principles of popular Christian parenting books, so we conducted an informal survey with open-ended questions and invited adult children and parents to share their perspectives. We also interviewed some of the respondents. One thing quickly became clear: People felt betrayed by these teachings. We have included excerpts from the survey responses and interviews throughout the book; these are published with the participants' permission. Minor adjustments have been made to some of the survey responses in the interest of readability and clarity.

Many parents who had worked hard to raise their children "the Christian way" were now experiencing guilt, shame, anger, or worry that they had done it all wrong. Adult children, wrestling with Christian ideals about honoring parents, struggled to separate and set boundaries. Many were grieving or angry, and others described difficulty cultivating authentic relationships with their parents. Some were simply hoping for an "I'm sorry" or an "I hear you." As Gen-Xers, millennials, and Gen Z began parenting, they found their childhoods reframed afresh and wanted a new way forward. We heard story after story of deep regret, painful and confusing relationship patterns, and confusion about God and faith.

Clearly, this is a long overdue conversation. Here at the outset, let us just say that we are so glad you are joining us.

We are both Christians who were raised in Christian families. Our own experiences overlap with some of the dynamics we explore in this book and give us adjacent familiarity with others. Though you won't find us processing our personal stories in these pages, we recognize how valuable and vulnerable it is to revisit childhood and grapple with family of origin dynamics. We are also both mothers who know well the exquisite joy and grace of parenthood intermingled with the potent blend of good intentions and inevitable shortcomings, of things done and things left undone, and the difficulty of reckoning with the reality of limitations and failures.

We are Christians, daughters, mothers, and wives, which means that we approach this work with a posture of compassion and curiosity and a desire to help families find new ways forward. We intend to tell the story of American evangelical parenting practices, and we believe understanding this collective history is a worthwhile endeavor all on its own. But *because* we are talking about family dynamics, we anticipate that this book will impact people personally as well.

We also recognize that some readers may no longer identify as Christians. Please know that you are welcome here. In the same way that this book is not about our personal parenting journeys or our childhoods, we are also not positioning ourselves to offer pastoral advice or become parenting experts. While we both have parenting experience and opinions, we recognize they are merely *our experiences and opinions*, which we believe are best shared in personal contexts.

What *do* we intend to offer? In these pages, you will find a general timeline of how ideas developed, common ingredients of Christian parenting myths, and observations about the impact they had on many people. We anticipate that you will have multiple "Aha!" light bulb moments, and we hope that you feel seen as you read this book.

INTRODUCTION

Pick up any Christian parenting book and you will likely find this verse from Proverbs prominently displayed: "Train up a child in the way he should go: and when he is old, he will not depart from it" (22:6 KJV). Many parents in the thick of raising young children read this passage as a command: "My job is to train up my child in a certain way." Devout parents of "prodigals" might see a sliver of hope that adult children who no longer espouse the Christian faith will someday return to the fold.

Christian parenting resources depend on promises made to parents: If you get it *right*, then there will be desired results—if not now, then somewhere down the road. The potent expectation for children to be discipled into right belief and right practice from infancy on up keeps families working hard, powered by everything from board books about systematic theology to prayer guides for grandparents.

Christian "experts"—often self-credentialed and self-platformed—explain how to bring meaning to the mundane, to wrangle the chaos of family life, to "do" parenting with excellence. The dedication in Justin Whitmel Earley's award-winning book *Habits of the Household* sums up the logic here: "It is easier to raise strong children than to repair broken men and women."[1] This statement shows up in multiple parenting resources. It powerfully showcases the parental longing to protect children from grief and keep them "unbroken."

Echoes of this concern can be found in statements such as this: "I had grown up in such a chaotic and abusive household that when I became a Christian as an adult, I was desperate to know how to parent the Christian way. I knew I didn't want to repeat my own experience. A friend handed me *Dare to Discipline*."[2] Many Christian parents wanted to know: If there is a right way to go, how can I make sure my children and I are on it? Countless Christian pastor-teachers lined up to answer this question, building empires along the way.

Gary and Anne Marie Ezzo, best known for their book *On Becoming Baby Wise* (1993) and their *Growing Kids God's Way* (1996) curriculum, demonstrate what it looks like to build a Christian parenting empire. Gary received an MA in ministry through Talbot School of Theology's program for adults without an undergraduate education, and Anne Marie had trained as a nurse. In 1984, they met "with a young couple with a three-month-old and a list of parenting questions."[3] As the Ezzos tell the story, they began to meet with other parents in their living room, and interest snowballed. They started teaching parenting classes at Grace Community Church (GCC), pastored by John MacArthur. The support of MacArthur's Grace to You ministry as well as access to GCC mailing lists and potential customers opened additional doors. At the peak of the Ezzos' influence (the early to mid-1990s), their programs were translated into seventeen languages and used in ninety-three countries, with seventy-thousand parents attending classes each week, and they now claim to have reached two million households.[4]

Numerous parenting books from this era include Gary Ezzo's coveted endorsement on the back cover, where his name lent credibility. Yet since the late 1990s, the Ezzos' work has come under scrutiny, leading even MacArthur to distance himself from their program. Critics cite allegations of authoritarian and domineering leadership, dismissal from multiple churches,[5] reported estrangement from adult children,[6] and objections from external sources like the American Academy of Pediatrics.[7] Even so, a thirtieth anniversary edition of *Baby Wise* came out in 2020, and the Growing Families brand still reaches readers worldwide.

Social media has allowed marketing-savvy Christian writers and communicators to capitalize on smaller built-in audiences. For example, the 2024 Fight, Laugh, Feast[8] family-life conference sold endorsement opportunities for anywhere from $500 to $5,000 in addition to tiered streaming and merchandise. For a price, anyone could have their logo displayed near the beverage station or have their organization boosted from the stage and so gain credibility with attendees. The most successful empires present themselves as an in-house, trusted, one-stop shop for every member of the family. Fight, Laugh, Feast is affiliated with Canon Press, the global media arm of pastor Douglas Wilson's empire, which includes a K–12 school, a classical education curriculum press, a university, a publishing house, and all the resulting revenue.

Some empire builders have more substantive credentials than others, but that is almost always inconsequential. James Dobson may have started his career by highlighting the "Dr." before his name, but his organization, Focus on the Family, grew into an empire in large part because of his strategic marketing and winsome persona. The Ezzos have no relevant credentials, but their endorsements were still welcome because they successfully sold books and became household names in Christian circles. We also see this in the desire of some parents to know what Christian celebrities have to say about any given topic. Well-known pastors like MacArthur can produce a parenting book, regardless of knowledge about parenting philosophies or evidence-based approaches.

Many Christian parenting experts assume that successful families all look the same. Resources presume a nuclear family with two married parents, so there is rarely mention of single, divorced, or widowed parents—or extended family members taking on parental roles. Most authors don't address neurodivergence or disability, even adjusting for awareness at the time of writing. The majority of the most influential evangelical parenting experts are White; this was the case when Christian parenting empires began forming in the 1970s, and it is still true today. The relative racial homogeneity of both the publishing industry and American evangelical institutions and organizations shows up in the Christian parenting book market, which has largely been dominated by White evangelical men.[9] Since the turn of the century, an increasing share of parenting content has been created by women, who have been able to leverage success on online platforms like Instagram to secure book deals, but there remains little racial diversity in the sector when it comes to traditional Christian publishing. While many of the authors in this niche would likely say that their advice is "biblical" and thus applicable across racial, socioeconomic, and geographic boundaries, as we will see, each author's background, experience, ideologies, and assumptions shape their parenting advice.

As the two of us examined over a hundred resources that spanned decades, we noticed that many of their marketing pitches hit the same notes. One after another, we found what we call "prosperity gospel parenting promises." These are claims that suggest that if parents approach parenting the right way, God will bless their efforts and obedience with happy, healthy, godly children who will testify to both parental faithfulness and the Christian way of life. This myth—that God provides a formula for "good Christian parenting"—permeates these resources, presenting an aspirational goal while also motivating parents with high eternal stakes.

We will examine various elements of these myths throughout this book, but for now we want to underscore that empire builders boosted their credibility with claims to teach the simple truths of the Bible. Many evangelicals trust a spiritual leader's authoritative teaching on every topic, especially when it comes with warnings like this one from *Growing Kids God's Way*: "God pre-programmed all factors for success into His divine plan. As with all matters discussed in Scripture, if you violate the principles, you forfeit the blessings. When you embrace His commandments, the blessings of joy and fulfillment will be yours."[10]

What parent wants to forfeit God's blessings or risk fearful outcomes? Spiritual goals can put anxious parents on an endless treadmill of introspection, leaving them wondering, "If Christ really changes everything, how does he change potty training? What does the gospel have to say about this?"[11] Because if the gospel has something specific to "say" about every area of life, then people must figure out what it is and do it.

When promised everything from godly children to a happy home, evangelical parents had a choice: trustingly comply or risk their children's spiritual well-being. And because much of the teaching relied on theological claims, it came with stowaway doctrines that shaped people's perspectives about the nature and character of God. This impacted individuals' spiritual formation, and it also intersected with the cultures of Christian communities and church families. The effects were both far-reaching and intensely personal. We recognize that for many readers our undertaking is no theoretical enterprise and speaks to the tenderest of places.

With that in mind, we have organized this book in such a way that it gives the reader a comprehensive understanding of the historical, sociological, and theological influences that undergird Christian parenting teaching. We recommend reading the chapters sequentially, but they are also accessible topically should you find yourself drawn to certain elements that align with your own experience.

We hope that this book will be a resource that equips readers who are actively parenting to weave together their own beliefs and personality with the individual needs and desires of the children who have been entrusted to their care. For parents who want to chart a new way forward through the ocean of Christian parenting resources, part 3 and the appendix offer suggestions for evaluating resources to determine whether they might serve your family well.

For those who come to this book wondering if we seek to tear down the church or to attack Christians, we invite you to give us an open-eyed read. It is our love for the church and for the truth that motivates us to scrutinize the biblical and theological underpinnings (or their lack thereof) in these resources. Because Christian parenting advice was often paired with spiritual authority language, claims were made *for* and *about* God. Families weren't just given advice; they were told God wanted them to do various things, and we believe it's important to question problematic Christian teaching. We have worked hard to do so with truthfulness, charity, and a desire to evaluate content using the metric of the life, ministry, and teaching of Jesus.

For those who come to this book as adult children or parents seeking to understand painful dynamics within their own lives, we see you. A difficult piece of this work is recognizing that many of these teachings betrayed entire families, resulting in anger, grief, and lament. There is no recouping the cost, and there is no way to go back and reclaim what might have been. But there is a way to restore agency to people who are attempting to navigate what is, and we hope that our work will help you as you travel along that path.

For those who come to this book after loss of faith, who are doing the difficult and painful work of deconstruction and detangling, or who may just be holding on to the last shred of hope, we see you too. Many Christian parenting resources position parents and other authority figures as mediators between children and God. We won't be doing that here; we entrust you to the God we believe relates to people directly, personally, and in ways where people are found and fully known.

For all others who come with tender memories, with the things that happened behind closed doors, with the grief and joys known only to their own hearts, know that you are beloved and dear children of God. Thank you for joining us here in these pages.

Part 1

How Did We Get Here?

The Builders of the Christian Parenting Empire

1

THE RIGHT KIND OF PARENTS

Creating the Christian Parenting Resource Market

Professor Harold Hill had to create a problem in order to sell a solution. The shifty protagonist of the musical comedy *The Music Man* knew it had to be a problem that the parents of River City would care about. They had to care enough not only to listen but also to trust and invest their time and money in the absurd solution he was about to propose: a boys' marching band.

"We got *trouble*, right here in River City!" he cried, pointing to the billiard parlor, where a newly installed pool table threatened to send young boys down the path of crude language, beer, and ragtime.

Hill's rousing appeal to unwitting customers was that the boys were at risk of becoming hooligans, and he had the perfect solution. After he established the enemy (the new pool table) and the danger (hooliganism), he turned to the crowd of mothers and fathers and said earnestly, "Now I know you folks are the right kind of parents . . ."[1]

The right kind of parents. Almost every parent wants to be the right kind of parent. Not just a good parent but the best parent they can be. And every parent can relate to the feeling of taking an infant home and sensing the crushing weight of responsibility that accompanies their joy and excitement. This unrelenting pressure sends parents to books, podcasts, blogs, and influencers. To be sure, not every parenting expert is a crook or scam artist, but even the most well-meaning self-appointed writers, coaches, and teachers sometimes exploit parental fears.

Many parents feel there is trouble lurking everywhere, that every day with their new baby is an opportunity either to get it right or to fail. They feel constantly at risk of being too permissive, too authoritarian, too involved, too hands-off. And many experts, both Christian and not, convince readers that parents are tragically underprepared for what lies ahead.

The stakes feel especially high for Christian parents. They may not be explicitly taught that children—their behavior, health, or salvation—directly reflect a parent's own spiritual goodness, but some come to believe it. Fear and the fervent desire to be the right kind of parents makes people desperate for answers, promises, and a guarantee that their kids will be okay.

The Discovery of Childhood: Parenting Advice in Nineteenth-Century America

Parental anxiety is nothing new. Every generation of parents and grandparents looks at the children around them and may be tempted to think, *What's wrong with the kids these days?* In Christian contexts, this concern can take on a panicked tone, often instigated by pastors writing about the nature of the parent-child relationship. A diverse library of historical texts, written across centuries and traditions, shapes the theological beliefs we have about children and families today.[2] Augustine of Hippo, writing in the late fourth century, imagined the jealous nature of babies based on his observations of nursing infants.[3] Puritan minister Cotton Mather wrote about the spiritual and practical duties of parents in *Cares About the Nursery* (1702).[4] Eighteenth-century revivalist and founder of Methodism John Wesley wrote and preached about child-rearing and published his mother's letter on the subject.[5] Christian thinkers discuss everything from the salvation of children to the development of self-control by a strictly regimented feeding schedule. Their concerns reflect the realities of daily life in their particular context.

In the 1800s, American Protestants played a central role in growing the publishing industry. During the first half of the century, evangelical publishers[6] "pioneered advances in paper-making, power printing, mass production, and corporate communication," and by 1855 they accounted for 16 percent of all books published in the United States.[7] The market was somewhat divided by various denominational publishers; even still, the "evangelical ecumenism" of figures like Dwight L. Moody won out as "the heart of a commercialism that became the operating logic for a new evangelical book industry."[8]

In nineteenth-century America, the Sunday school movement[9] and revivalism spurred interest in family-life teaching. Ministers were still the most trusted figures when it came to parenting advice, but their position in American society was shifting, as was the tone of their messages. Children spent most of their time in the home, and so the "little church" of the domestic sphere was seen as the primary locus for spiritual formation. Henry Clay Trumbull, editor of *The Sunday-School Times* and a missionary for the Sunday and Adult School Union (and great-grandfather of Elisabeth Elliot, a notable author in her own right), wrote *Hints on Child Training* in 1890, recognizing that many American parents considered raising children to be a spiritual duty.

One serial publication contained essays from clergy offering parenting advice, with titles like "Parental Duties." In one issue, the editor included a call for guest essays from "successful" parents. It's an early example of interest in Christian parenting advice from people whose only authority was their record of raising good Christian children: "We respectfully solicit communications for publication in this work, from those parents who have been successful in the moral and religious training of their children, detailing with some particularity, the course pursued. This publication will afford such parents an opportunity to speak to *twenty-five or thirty thousand* persons."[10] Parenting experience alone could draw a large, diverse crowd.

On the next page of the publication, the Reverend Jacob Abbott entreated parents to develop character and a tender conscience in their children, so that they might eventually become sensitive to the Holy Spirit.[11] Abbott warned readers that *too much* religious instruction might alienate children and reminded parents that coldness, harsh words, or impatience would negatively impact their children more than any lecture. Abbott's essay and other instructions of the time assume that a respectable American parent was a *Christian* parent, eager to see their children grow into God-fearing citizens.

The turn of the twentieth century brought what historians refer to as a "discovery" of childhood.[12] When *Children: The Magazine for Parents* (later retitled *Parents Magazine*) launched in 1926, its editors assured parents that they could help them navigate the modern world, covering topics from psychology to nutrition. In the premier issue, the editors announced that their aim was "to bring you who are out on the firing-line, the scientific findings of specialists concerning the child's needs of mind, body, and spirit from birth to the twenty-first year.

We hope to set them before you with simplicity and sympathy, with humor and understanding. . . . It is a new world of loving understanding, wise tolerance and humility into which today's pioneers in child study lead us."[13]

In the seventy-five years between Abbott's essay and the first issue of *Children*, American life had evolved on all fronts. The nation had weathered a civil war, the Industrial Revolution, and World War I. Women had won the vote. The temperance movement was in full swing. In 1849, elementary schooling was not compulsory in any of the states; by 1917, it was universally required. In the twentieth century, children were spending more time away from their homes than ever before. Interest in education research and child psychology had grown, due in part to figures like John Dewey and Sigmund Freud. The early twentieth century also saw new research on child development, psychology, and sociology, which promised professionals and parents new best practices for child-rearing and care. Parents increasingly looked to this new army of experts rather than religious leaders to know how best to mold their children.

The Parenting Book Boom

Historian Peter Stearns identifies the launch of *Children*, as well as the growing popularity of child-rearing books in the 1920s, as the beginning of the parenting book boom. He links this to the increase in polling in the 1930s, which made it possible to measure public opinion and attitudes—including parental concerns. This also raised social awareness of *hypothetical* concerns, hinting to parents that, if they weren't already, they *should* be worried about things like too much television, too much physical exercise or not enough, or whether children were drinking enough milk.[14] Just as concerns about children's welfare were on the rise (with protection from labor abuses, increased vaccination and better health care, and accessible education), so were parents' anxieties.[15]

The wide-ranging genre of books known as "self-help" had gained widespread traction since the mid-nineteenth century due to the public fascination with millionaires and the "secrets" they must have known in order to amass their fortunes. Most early self-help books were about how to get rich. In 1913, G. K. Chesterton bemoaned the popularity of the growing genre in an essay titled "The Fallacy of Success." Chesterton wryly observed, "That a thing is successful merely means that it is; a millionaire is successful in being a millionaire and a donkey in being a donkey."[16] The only thing we can know about a millionaire's success, he insisted, is that he *is* a millionaire. Offering secret knowledge about how to become successful, Chesterton wrote, "is not mere business; it is not even mere cynicism. It is mysticism."[17] "Mysticism" here is what modern readers might recognize as *manifesting*, which is the idea that someone can wish something into being or look to the universe to offer it to them. This magical thinking still characterizes many self-help books that promise quick fixes, hacks, secret knowledge, and "one weird trick" related to anything from weight loss to dating.

It makes perfect sense that the self-help genre would eventually encompass parenting resources. Parenting can be hard, unpredictable, and isolating, and self-help books offer an abstract community and the feeling of being seen.[18] A mother with a newborn might feel understood and affirmed when she reads a book about breastfeeding or infant care. A book about discipline or "strong-willed" children might encourage a father, isolated in his struggle with anger at his toddler's erratic behavior. Desperate parents of teenagers might want help navigating their teen's social-media obsession. Parents often struggle with shame and difficulty admitting their shortcomings. Experiencing anger or resentment as a parent can feel like utter failure, and parenting books offer solutions to parents who are having a hard time and don't have a safe place to ask questions or talk openly about their problems.

Many parents would rather order a book online than admit to someone in their family or inner circle that they feel like they are failing with their child. A parent who follows an influencer might find comfort in getting advice from a faraway, seemingly put-together figure who can't judge or question their private choices. But the rise in available resources has arguably driven *more* anxiety, not less.

Historian Ann Hulbert notes in her book *Raising America* that five times as many parenting books were published in 1997 than in 1975.[19] The baby boom, economic growth and prosperity, and an increase in research and information about child development meant that parents had more money and time to spend learning about the best practices of child-rearing, according to the most cutting-edge research. Parents who felt that they may have been raised with outdated and potentially harmful methods could find new resources and products that would help them to do it better, to get it *right*.

Parents looking to give their kids a head start in the late 1990s and early 2000s flocked to Baby Einstein products. The brand grew from a homemade video made by Julie Aigner-Clark in 1996 to a company purchased by Disney for $25 million five years later.[20] Baby Einstein marketers claimed their toys, books, and DVDs stimulated babies' brains, made them smarter, and set them on an early path to literacy. It didn't take long for the shine to wear off as consumers learned how little research supported their claims and how overuse of the products might have adverse effects.[21] A chorus of concerns quickly grew loud enough to force refunds and lawsuits, but not before Baby Einstein earned millions of dollars and made up almost 90 percent of the baby media market.

Marketing to parents almost always includes promises. Any list of best-selling parenting books reveals the top-of-mind parental concerns of the day: baby brain development, helping children become resilient, kids and diet culture, working during pregnancy, sleep difficulties, or dealing with screen time and mental health. Christian families add their child's salvation and spiritual health to the list. Many Christian parenting books heightened parental anxiety by suggesting that parents could not trust their own instincts and needed to carefully navigate an ocean of information to find the *right* formula for success.

Parenting experts in the Christian niche and in the mainstream have convinced generations of parents that they should be constantly improving and that they need *lots* of help. Insecure parents are also willing to *buy* things, and in so doing help launch the careers and platforms of those with a compelling message.

Daring Disciplinarians

The modern market for Christian parenting resources was born when one expert dared to answer a perennial parenting question, "More discipline or more nurture?" with a resounding *more discipline*!

James Dobson insisted that the mainstream advice of the previous two decades from figures like Dr. Benjamin Spock—whose adage was "trust yourself, you know more than you think you do"—was not only inadequate but also wreaking havoc on American families. Dobson's 1970 best-selling book *Dare to Discipline* was the first of many books on parenting, family life, and the moral crisis in America. With a PhD in psychology, Dobson positioned himself as a prophetic outsider, standing up to his mainstream contemporaries in order to put families back on track. He gestured to the social and political turmoil of the 1960s and '70s and issued warnings to parents to look at what decades of foolish parenting advice had brought about.

Dobson offered solutions in the form of "biblical" guidance. As he said in one interview, "I'm drawing on Somebody else's ideas and that Somebody doesn't make mistakes."[22] Setting the stage for omnicompetent evangelical pastor-teachers of the coming decades, Dobson presented himself as someone who could correctly interpret the Bible and the state of the world and in turn communicate God's ideas about parenting and family life.

"The institutions of marriage and parenthood were not the inventions of mere men and women," Dobson wrote in his 1976 book *Family Under Fire*. Rather, marriage and the family unit were "created and sanctioned by God Almighty," he continued, before warning, "If we deviate from His plan . . . we will witness (I believe) the disintegration of everything of value and meaning. . . . To tamper with the ground floor is to threaten the entire superstructure!"[23] For Christian parents, being the right kind of parent included accountability to God for their parenting decisions. Dobson raised the stakes of being an obedient Christian parent: Civilization would crumble if they didn't course-correct.

Dobson opened the first chapter of *Dare to Discipline* with an anecdote about Mrs. Nichols and her three-year-old daughter, Sandy, whom he described as "defiant," "a tyrant and a dictator," and "not accustomed to doing anything she doesn't want to do," because she had a meltdown over a glass of water. Dobson concluded that both the parent and the child were "among the many casualties of an unworkable, illogical philosophy of child management" that "dominated" the recent literature on the subject.[24]

Dobson was certainly not the first to suggest that kids these days have no discipline and no respect for authority, but his message found an eager and anxious audience. Christian parents, alongside their secular peers, were disturbed by images of campus protests, draft-card burnings, and Woodstock. They were desperate for advice about raising well-behaved citizens and wanted to keep their children safe in a dangerous world.

Benjamin Spock, the famous child-rearing expert of the mid-twentieth century, advocated flexibility and a "connected" approach to raising children. But by today's standards, his teachings on discipline read as rather strict. He taught the value of consistent discipline, saying that spanking was "less poisonous than lengthy disapproval, because it clears the air, for parent and child."[25] Spanking was still common in the majority of American families in the 1960s and '70s, yet Dobson was convinced that American parents were too heavy on love and too light on discipline.[26]

Dobson claimed that the movement away from discipline disempowered parents, who had regrettably learned that "all forms of punishment were harmful and unfair." He bemoaned the "unfortunate imbalance" in homes where the "happy theory of 'permissive democracy'" had taken over. "We have sacrificed this generation on the altar of overindulgence, permissiveness, and smother-love," he concluded.[27]

Dobson's diagnosis failed to acknowledge key shifts in American families following World War II. For example, he doesn't discuss the new freedoms of the 1940s, when teenagers had unprecedented levels of independence as they entered the workforce alongside many of their mothers. The war created a labor force that granted many women and teens autonomy and purchasing power outside the home. During the 1940s, "whether in response to the threats of the adult world's war or the stress of family disruption, adolescents took on a new and distinctive social identity, independent of their parents," and "parents grew more conscious than ever before that teenagers had been liberated from adult control."[28]

Dobson glosses over the intense upheaval of the twentieth century. After the war, American life became more family-centric as the baby boom and economic prosperity reshaped the way US citizens expected to live, play, and work. But rather than consider how the social, economic, and political changes of the previous decade affected family life, Dobson zeroed in on the need for more discipline. This included discipline in the schools. *Dare to Discipline* devotes several chapters to empowering teachers to properly maintain order in the classroom.

It is worth highlighting that Dobson's own parenting experiences feature prominently in his later books, yet at the time he was forming his viewpoints he was a brand-new father. Dobson wrote *Dare to Discipline* soon after finishing his doctoral studies, while working as a youth counselor to "450 disrespectful, haughty ninth graders," whom he described as "the forerunners of the hostile, aggressive, drug-using teen-agers seen in many high schools today."[29]

Dobson also worked under Paul Popenoe, one of the first figures in the field of marriage counseling to attempt a scientific approach to helping families ensure successful marriages and family life. Popenoe, who wrote *Modern Marriage: A Handbook* (1925) and *Can This Marriage Be Saved?* (1960), was an atheist and a eugenicist who founded the American Institute of Family Relations in part to "remove what he thought to be obstacles to white reproduction."[30] Popenoe wanted to build up the nuclear family as a means of restoring social order,[31] and in the foreword he wrote for the first edition of *Dare to Discipline*, he reassured parents that "readers who follow [Dobson] will find that they get the results they want."[32]

At the foundation of Dobson's successful empire is this imperative: Parents must exercise and protect their authority, and children must obey. Without both parents and children playing their rightful part, society would crumble. Dobson was convinced that the practices of parents in the 1950s had produced the generation that protested the Vietnam War, experimented with drugs, and had premarital sex. Dobson's message was timely. It spoke to terrified parents who worried about what they saw in the news and in the entertainment media enjoyed by their children.

Dare to Discipline sold more than two million copies in its first seven years on the market. The book was not particularly focused on the Christian faith (although a chapter titled "A Moment for Mom" does offer a two-page discussion of "the rod" in Proverbs), but Dobson, as the son and grandson of Church of the Nazarene preachers, showed an innate ability to gain the trust of his audience. He went on to hone his skills on the speaking circuit, both in auditoriums and over the airwaves. In 1978, Dobson released the video series Building a Family Legacy, which was reportedly viewed by over one hundred million people in the following decade.[33] Dobson's knack for public speaking and capturing an audience, combined with an ambitious media output, soon made him a respected voice on family life among American evangelicals.

A contrasting Christian public figure whose communication skills made him a household name among families was Fred Rogers, a Presbyterian minister who created the television program *Mister Rogers' Neighborhood*, which aired on public television from 1968 until 2001. Rogers responded to the social upheaval of the time by addressing children directly and emphasizing the importance of community relationships rather than focusing on the primacy of the nuclear family unit, as Dobson did.

Dobson founded Focus on the Family in 1977. Over the next two decades, this organization grew into a politically powerful institution. When it opened its Colorado Springs headquarters in 1994, it was given its own postal code due to the thousands of letters that poured in from Christians looking for biblical advice on family life.[34] In 1999, Focus on the Family executives reported that twelve thousand people a day called or wrote to the organization asking for guidance and resources, and they claimed that its radio broadcasts reached "easily a billion" listeners worldwide (including six hundred million in China).[35] At the dawn of the new millennium, secular broadcasters like ABC were courting Dobson for a short radio spot. He had secured an audience well beyond evangelicals and conservative Christians.

Before Dobson, Christian pastors and counselors wrote books about children and parenting—Clyde Narramore's *Discipline in the Christian Home* (1961) and David and Virginia Edens' *Why God Gave Children Parents* (1966) are two examples—but none had managed to leverage their persona and message to build a media empire. Like Billy Graham did with his evangelistic crusades, Dobson understood how to package his message to captivate the hearts of Christians and spiritually curious listeners and viewers from a variety of backgrounds. The two men came to occupy a tier of White American evangelical leadership that few after them would reach. Graham preached salvation for the individual. Dobson preached salvation for the family.

Today's landscape of Christian parenting books and media is far more diffuse than it was fifty years ago, but its writers and teachers preach a familiar message. It's a message about *biblical* parenting and so benefits from the appearance of timelessness. But no Christian parenting expert writes in a vacuum. Labeling parenting advice "Christian" or "biblical" may help sell books, but it also obscures the social and political forces that motivated their authors. The Christian parenting book market grew alongside the coalition of the Religious Right, something we need to explore in order to understand how reactionary politics and biblical parenting continue to shape American evangelical families.

2

THE BIBLE TELLS US SO

Authors, Influencers, and the Politics of Set-Apart Parenthood

I (Kelsey) am scrolling through Instagram, exploring the content of a popular parenting influencer. Posts feature carefully chosen font combinations, muted color palettes, and encouraging Bible verses. The algorithm serves me a video of two children hiking through a rugged landscape peppered with patches of snow; the wind whips their hair across their faces. The text says, "God calls us to exercise authority over our children . . . but authority like Jesus models it." In the caption, the content creator writes, "Biblical authority certainly has rules. There are consequences for sin . . . even painful consequences! We as adults have consequences for sin in our lives! BUT. [Discipline] is done in the context of a loving relationship."[1] At the bottom of the post is a hashtag with the title of an enduringly popular Christian parenting book: #shepherdingachildsheart.

As we were researching for this book, we saw multiple churches advertise parenting classes involving Tedd Tripp's

1995 bestseller *Shepherding a Child's Heart*. Just as *The Purpose Driven Life* and *My Utmost for His Highest* and *Mere Christianity* have become "Christian living" classics, so the parenting niche has its own short list of tried-and-true resources. The books are gifted and regifted, and communities circulate the ideas in them like folk wisdom.

Outside the Christian world, parenting books don't have much staying power across generations. Parents are always looking for resources based on the latest information and research. For a parenting book to have staying power, it has to be perceived as timeless. Something about its content and author must promise that no matter the era or location, *these* truths about parenting remain the same (and this author has figured out what those truths are).

This is perhaps why Christian parenting books like *Shepherding a Child's Heart* stay in circulation. Tripp appeals to parents by insisting that his approach is, above all else, *biblical*. Scripture doesn't change, so God's advice to parents doesn't change. The authors of Christian parenting books have long framed their advice and ideas as "biblical"—a label that gives the impression of authorial neutrality, positioning them as mouthpieces for God's word.

In 1994, Zondervan published *The Parenting Bible*, an NIV study Bible with notes and book excerpts by prominent figures in the Christian parenting and family-life sphere: Tim Kimmel (author of *A Legacy of Love*), Chuck Swindoll, Bruce Narramore, and James Dobson represent a sampling. The publication of *The Parenting Bible* shows how marketable Christian parenting advice had become by the early '90s. It also demonstrates that, for Christian parents, the right advice from the right person was, above all, biblical. Biblical parenting advice was functionally a Bible commentary, guiding the application of Scripture to child-rearing.

Before we go further, it's worth stating that it's impossible to evaluate the motivations of any Christian parenting expert;

some, surely, are well-intentioned and believe that what they are presenting is, in fact, biblical. But when devotional sincerity gets wrapped up in expanding ministry empires, book sales, and clickbait income, it's reasonable to assume that multiple motives and incentives shape the product.

The word "biblical" can obscure the ideological and political motivations of those offering parenting advice. Some parenting experts use this label to give their teaching the appearance of scriptural authority, even if they are sharing personal experiences and preferences.

James Dobson supported his guidance by insisting that he wasn't promoting his own ideas but God's.[2] The back cover of John MacArthur's 2000 book, *What the Bible Says About Parenting: God's Plan for Rearing Your Child*, claims that the book simply presents "the principles of biblical parenting with as much clarity as possible." John Rosemond followed up *Parenting by the Book: Biblical Wisdom for Raising Your Child* (2007) with *The Bible Parenting Code: Revealing God's Perfect Parenting Plan* (2021). Countless other resources include titles, subtitles, or biblical allusions that assert that if parents follow *their* advice, they will discover and practice what the Bible *really* says about parenting.

For many evangelicals, "biblical" is more than a label; it's an ideology. It signals a commitment to a particular way of interpreting Scripture as an integral part of a *truly* Christian worldview. Political philosopher Jason Blakely describes "ideology" as a map we use to help us navigate the world but which we can end up mistaking for the landscape itself.[3] We can allow ourselves to be so immersed in ideology that it becomes our world. For some evangelicals, commitment to a particular approach to the Bible *is* the whole of Christian faith. To label a book, piece of advice, or parenting method biblical is to acknowledge a shared ideological project, one that sets evangelicals apart from other Christians or even other Protestant groups with shared Scripture and history.

In the Christian parenting book and content market, the word "biblical" has become a stand-in for a constellation of ideas and political commitments. In the 1970s and '80s, it became a watchword for political conservatives who advocated for family values and built the coalition that became the Christian Right. Today, for evangelicals who speak the correct insider-Christianese, the word "biblical" signals belief in a particular approach to Scripture *and* a particular posture of countercultural vigilance. To practice "biblical parenting" is to be the right kind of parent and the right kind of Christian.

Today, the influencer sphere of social media has become the go-to place for Christian parents to immerse themselves in a biblical perspective. Although the term "influencer" is relatively new, it describes what successful teachers and writers have been doing for decades. A Christian influencer uses their lifestyle and identity to sell their brand, content, and version of lived Christianity.[4] The aesthetics and technology of platforms like Instagram, Facebook, and TikTok are twenty-first-century innovations, but many "new experts" in these digital spaces are repackaging and adapting the ideas and teaching of Tedd Tripp, James Dobson, Larry Christenson, Chuck Swindoll, Ginger Hubbard, and Gary Ezzo as if the historical context they came from doesn't matter. After all, biblical parenting advice is timeless, tried and true. Right?

The Importance of Inerrancy

American Christians have long tussled over who has the authority to interpret the Bible. Since the late nineteenth century, Christian fundamentalists and evangelicals have defended their reading of Scripture against conflicting appraisals from modern biblical scholars. Evangelical theologian J. I. Packer, a key signer and advocate of the 1978 Chicago Statement on Inerrancy, argued that "as soon as you convict Scripture of making the smallest mistakes you start to abandon both the biblical understanding of biblical inspiration and also the systematic functioning of the Bible as the organ of God's authority, his rightful and effective rule over his people's faith and life."[5]

Inerrancy, as commonly understood, claims that the Bible is without error, authoritative, and understandable. This view offers evangelicals confidence and assurance that a "common sense"[6] reading of Scripture will help them to discern the value of almost anything. Devotion to inerrancy and reverence for the Bible's authority compel people to view Scripture as a kind of instruction manual for every area of life.

In the late 1960s, Presbyterian pastor Jay Adams was dismayed by what he saw as unbiblical, dangerous, and ineffective dimensions of modern psychology. He developed an alternative framework he called "nouthetic counseling"[7] (widely known today as "biblical counseling"). When Adams published *Competent to Counsel* in 1970, he wanted to equip pastors to source the Bible so they could help laypeople navigate any kind of problem by "putting off" sin and "putting on" right living. Adams functionally expanded the Christian doctrines of perspicuity and sufficiency—that Scripture is clear and authoritative—in such a way that the Bible became primarily a comprehensive rule book for right living. He also cast suspicion on external sources of authority, particularly secular ones, and taught that Christians could consult the Bible alone for every situation.

Today, Bob Jones University, John MacArthur's Grace Community Church, and numerous other churches and seminaries offer in-house biblical counseling to families in crisis based on Adams's models. His original resources are still used as certification for the Association of Certified Biblical Counselors. They have been translated into multiple languages and pitched as accessible and inexpensive ways to train pastors globally. Tedd Tripp (who credits Adams and other biblical counseling pioneers in his acknowledgments) and Ginger Hubbard, two of the most popular parenting experts of the past three decades, rely heavily on nouthetic teaching, such that today's parents may find themselves parenting according to Adams's *interpretations* of Scripture, even while they may believe they are parenting according to Scripture alone.

At the heart of biblical counseling is behavioral change. Husbands and wives, mothers and fathers, and sons and daughters learn what is expected of them, with isolated Bible verses to support every admonition. The appeal is clear: Promised results offer measurable goals that can relieve the anxiety that comes from lack of control. If you quantify the problem in a measurable way, you can offer a solution. Biblical counseling was (and still is) offered in direct opposition to what are framed as secular, humanistic ideas about child development.

As mainline denominations experienced schisms over perceived departures from orthodoxy and orthopraxy, a shared understanding of biblical authority among evangelicals protected their faith, helped people chart out acceptable Christian practices, and offered a marker of insider/outsider status, which became important information as the culture wars intensified. Many Christian parenting experts enticed readers to their niche by stoking skepticism of mainstream wisdom, and they convinced parents they needed identifiably Christian parenting resources to help them navigate an increasingly hostile world. The algorithmic echo chambers of social media today only enhance this insularity and tribalism.

As the culture wars ramped up, some Christian leaders struck a confrontational, strident note. In the late 1960s, churches bused youth groups to sold-out stadiums for Bill Gothard's Institute in Basic Youth Conflicts seminars. Equipped with handouts and hours of lectures, teenagers learned Gothard's "biblical principles" for life. Parents learned how to establish their authority in the home. Families learned how to homeschool according to Gothard's curricula. Much like the content from

Dobson and Focus on the Family, Gothard's outlook appealed across denominational lines, took a multimedia approach, and spread the message by word of mouth. Theological distinctives paled next to family-life commitments based on "biblical" principles.

Gothard, whose influence extended across decades, wasn't the only one casting a prescriptive vision of the modern Christian family. Larry Christenson's *The Christian Family* (1970), translated into nine languages, was another widely distributed book of parental guidance. This book came with an endorsement from "Mrs. Billy Graham" (Ruth Bell Graham) and promised life-changing practices—ones he had implemented in his own home—for families facing the "prevailing pattern of relativism and permissiveness" in modern life. He explained how a church-led retreat had inspired parents to return to the Bible to discover "God's order for parents." Christenson wrote that he and his wife began to implement a biblical model of parenting and saw an "*overnight* . . . dramatic change."[8]

Christenson was relatively circumspect about offering parental guidance, insisting that he was not giving prescriptive tips and tricks but relaying general principles. However, the results he promised offered enticing overnight transformations and a quiet revolution in family life. You can hear echoes of this in the captions of social-media posts: "In our family we . . ." followed by enthusiastic testimonies of life-changing results. And no topic is off-limits. If the Bible offers plain, accessible, and authoritative advice for *every* area of life, then it follows that influencers (much like the pastor-teachers before them) can and *should* speak to social issues, current events, and politics.

Parenting Is Political

At a campaign rally in Georgia in the weeks leading up to the 2024 presidential election, conservative pundit Tucker Carlson riled up the crowd with a speech about Donald Trump and the return of fatherly authority. Carlson described the then-candidate as a stern father promising to administer a "vigorous spanking" to an unruly adolescent daughter as the crowd joined in with chants of "Daddy's home" and "Daddy Don."[9] In certain segments of today's America, people are primed for a message of law and order, just as they were in earlier tumultuous eras.

Ideas about parental authority and the importance of child obedience have been used by politicians to engage their base for decades. Dobson's book *Family Under Fire* (1976) outlines perceived attacks on the nuclear family and warns about anti-authoritarian tendencies in children and young adults.[10] Similar talking points punctuated the 1968 presidential campaign of Richard Nixon, who claimed that American youth were "overpowered, over-protected, and over-patronized" by adults who were "sheltering and coddling" them.[11] *Dare to Discipline* wasn't just about the Christian family; it was also about the need for more consistent, swift, and painful child discipline. America needed a return to law and order, starting in good Christian homes.

Dobson was more effective than any of his predecessors writing about the Christian family on one particular front: He made parenting political. He railed against child psychologists, educators, and parents who let children run wild and show blatant disrespect without delivering adequate consequences, *and* he linked their failures to the social upheaval of the time. Conservative evangelicals cast doubt on the work of Benjamin Spock, partly because he openly supported anti-Vietnam protesters. Authors like Larry Christenson, James Dobson, Tedd Tripp, Gary Ezzo, Chuck Swindoll, Bruce Narramore, and Kenneth Gangel, all of whom wrote books about biblical parenting and family life during the 1970s, '80s, and '90s, relied on hand-selected anecdotes and vignettes about parenting moments they had witnessed to convince readers that biblical parenting could help get American culture back on track.

The most popular Christian parenting experts of the late twentieth century were deeply concerned about the unrest of the 1960s and '70s and the political fallout of that period. Whether marketed as child-rearing manuals or books about the importance of Christian family life, their resources are filled with references to drugs, divorce rates, feminism, public disorder, crime, and lawless college campuses. Readers who weren't around for or don't remember that period might easily miss the political undertones or explicit nods to partisan politics, but references to family values, respect for authority, power hierarchies, and moral decline align with conservative talking points of that period.

Many anxious parents of the 1960s and '70s experienced the period as an apocalypse, and Christian parenting literature of the decades following comes with apocalyptic framing. Protests strained college campuses, integration changed public schooling, and the civil rights movement exposed deep racial rifts in the country (and in its churches). In addition, more libertine attitudes about sexual behavior were sure signs that the kids were unquestionably *not* all right. Dobson's stern message about discipline and order put him—and a cohort of other writers courting the same readership—in a position to benefit from and shape the message of the growing coalition that would become known as the Christian Right.[12]

Tim LaHaye, best known as the author of the Left Behind series, helped found the Republican-aligned Council for National Policy and the pro-family organization Concerned Women for America. He wrote several books about the threat of secular humanism and the decline of the American family. In 1980, he published *The Battle for the Mind*, followed by *The Battle for the Family* (1982) and *The Battle for the Public Schools* (1983), and went on to reach over one million families through his

Family Life seminars.[13] In the preface to *The Battle for the Family*, LaHaye claims to be writing on behalf of the "overwhelming majority of Americans" who hold to "traditional morals and values."[14] And in *The Battle for the Mind*, he argues that humanism is a new religion taking control of America and that the "moral majority" needs to take action.

Similarly, Larry Christenson framed faithful family life as a political and evangelistic project, writing in his 1970 book, *The Christian Family*, "Our country has never before experienced such flagrant disregard for law and order," and even "the most hardened pagan will sit up and take notice of a family which has learned to live well together—a family where the husband and wife show mutual love and respect, and the children are polite and well-behaved."[15]

While not as visibly politically active as Dobson or LaHaye, Christenson was an influential figure in the Lutheran renewal movement during the 1970s and '80s, which brought charismatic theology and practices into the mainline and strengthened ties to conservative political causes (like the pro-life movement) in some regional groups.[16] Adopting the language of law and order and family values, Christenson argued that social and political upheaval was a form of spiritual warfare and that the "divine order" of the Christian home was a stronghold: "Behind international conflict, behind social conflict, behind personal and family conflict lurks the Master Agitator, the Master String-Puller—Satan."[17]

In *The Family First* (1972), Kenneth Gangel (then-president of Miami Christian College) appraised the ill effects of urbanization, secularization, divorce, and the "Women's Liberation Movement." All of these had, in his view, contributed to an alarming decline in the health of American families. He wrote, "Some historians (both secular and Christian) have argued that the breakdown of the home was a problem in the corruption of Ancient Rome, and have written rather convincing parallels between the history of that society and the dissolution of family units in our own."[18]

Throughout his book, Gangel frames his analyses and advice with the term "biblical," writing in the prologue, "God doesn't play by our rules or march to the beat of earthly drummers. His truth is absolute. Secular sociologists may reject the family but the Heavenly Father still expects earthly fathers to pattern their homes after his Biblical blueprint."[19]

For Gangel, Christenson, and Dobson, the Christian family was a bulwark against moral decay that needed to be strengthened. The cultivation of Christian families was a form of political action against the "warped ethics which teach children and young people to expect something for nothing" (likely a coded critique of welfare) and "the equalization of the sexes screamed at television cameras by bra-less females searching for a role which they have already abandoned" (an explicit condemnation of second-wave feminism).[20]

As many historians have noted, the Christian Right was not a monolith. It included Catholics, evangelicals, and mainline Protestants who represented the more revivalist, often politically active wings of their denominations. Social concerns, rather than doctrine, provided adequate common ground between these otherwise disparate groups. Historian Margaret Bendroth observes that, in the twentieth century, "family values" became so strongly associated with the Christian Right that "many moderate and liberal Protestants have shied away from the phrase, reinforcing the assumption that only theologically and politically conservative Protestants are pro-family."[21] As liberal Protestants retreated from the discourse, those associated with the Christian Right (particularly evangelicals) became the authorities on child-rearing, flooding the market with books and media.

Among some conservative Christians, "biblical" has become synonymous with "countercultural," referring to the

Christian's call to fight against the corrupting forces of the world. Influenced by the frameworks of nouthetic counseling and inerrancy, they point to ambiguous adversaries like "the culture" or "the world" to convince Christian parents that they are fighting a war for their children. Many authors in the Christian parenting book niche avoid affiliating with a particular political party; instead, they lean into the reactionary rhetoric of counterculturalism. Some, like Gangel, clearly reference social issues like women's rights or divorce; others pull their punches or use veiled language that borrows from or harmonizes with the agenda of the Christian Right.

In their 1989 book, *Discovering Your Child's Design*, Ralph Mattson and Thom Black wrote, "As Christians, we might expect to be immune to the influence of current theories about why we and our children behave the way we do. After all, don't we base our child-rearing practices on biblical principles? Not always. Too often, without even knowing it, we yield to the influence of the world's confused way of looking at children."[22]

This kind of "Bible versus the world" rhetoric continues today, adjusting to the cultural concerns of the moment. Recently, while promoting his book *The War on Children: Providing Refuge for Your Children in a Hostile World* (2024), John MacArthur went viral for calling PTSD, ADHD, and OCD "noble lies," going on to say that "behavior is essentially the result of choices that kids make, and if you parent them properly they'll make right choices."[23] Social concerns—in this case, the overmedication of children—speak to suspicion of secular expertise and a desire for an easy answer that will help parents protect their children and ensure desirable outcomes.

To be clear, it's not as though evangelical leaders were inventing problems, nor were they the only ones expressing concerns about social change. Many Americans in the 1960s and '70s were rocked by the swiftly changing norms around gender, sex, divorce, and adolescence. Furthermore, popular books of the time, such as Kate Millet's *Sexual Politics* (1970) and David Cooper's *Death of the Family* (1972), seemed to question the value of the nuclear family unit. Today, Abigail Shrier's best-selling book, *Bad Therapy*, sounds an alarm similar to MacArthur's. Christian parenting experts are unique, however, in claiming to have parenting solutions directly from the Word of God that can fix societal problems.

Today, parents who are concerned about the state of the American family will find books, podcasts, vlogs, and social media from people who affirm their sense of urgency and reassure them: You're right, the world *is* upside down, and you need to protect your children. Many parents feel alarmed by gender wars, pandemic-era school closures and mask mandates, political polarization, and social media's ability to capture the time and attention of their children. Christians now, as in the past, must decide whether it is time for fight or flight. Should they further withdraw their families—their children—from the mainstream chaos or enter into a battle for the culture?

Influencers Take Up the Christian Parenting Mantle

The label "Christian parenting influencer" might seem dismissive when applied to someone who thinks of their social-media presence as a ministry. But "influencer" isn't a pejorative; it accurately captures Christian figures who use social media to grow their brand and reach, which may lead to opportunities to teach in churches or at conferences, write books, launch podcasts, or sell Bible studies and other merchandise. Discomfort with the term may reveal a healthy skepticism of people who wield spiritual influence via social media with little to no accountability.

As we discussed in the previous section, Christenson, Dobson, and Tripp instructed Christian parents to look for advice and guidance outside the mainstream. Today's Christian parenting influencers offer inspiration mixed with a trendy aesthetic and occasional wellness content, casting a vision of set-apart, countercultural parenthood. That vision isn't less political than that of their predecessors; it has simply met a different political moment.

Abbie Halberstadt, the author of *M Is for Mama: A Rebellion Against Mediocre Motherhood*, describes herself as a "Bible-believing Mother of 10" and has over two hundred thousand followers on Instagram and a popular podcast. She uses a familiar frame for her ideas: "I firmly believe that the Bible has given us clear principles to live by that can make this whole motherhood gig a lot less intimidating and isolating. . . . I have had enough practice applying some of [these] wise biblical principles . . . to get a pretty good feel for some of the strategies that are helpful to all mamas."[24] In addition to the Bible, she also draws on the advice of other women, including her mother, fellow mom friends, and well-known figures such as Sally Clarkson, Elisabeth Elliot, and Ruth Bell Graham.

Halberstadt shares parenting advice and also writes about household tasks, her kitchen remodel, and sponsored products. Her *M Is for Mama* podcast delivers "encouragement for all things motherhood," including "practical helps and systems" and "examinations of what the Bible has to say about social issues."[25] Halberstadt addresses politics and hot-button topics like whether not having kids is biblical, the pitfalls of fandom (via Taylor Swift), and deconstruction. She overtly links her faith to her conservative political commitments.

"My theology informs my politics, and because politics affect the culture, I don't take lightly my ability to 'be political' for the sake of influencing our culture toward righteousness," Halberstadt wrote in an Instagram post on November 4, 2024, the day before the US presidential election. She goes on to say that she prioritizes voting for candidates who value "pre-born life," parental rights ("particularly when it comes to children who wish to mutilate themselves in the name of gender dysphoria"), border policies that "emphasize proper procedures for immigration and protect our nation's citizens," and "personal responsibility for health" rather than "one-size-fits-all-mandates."[26] Much of the post echoes agreement with the Republican Party's agenda during the 2024 election.

The Christian parenting book market and conservative politics have been intertwined for decades, and the relationship goes both ways. Some conservative political leaders have carved out side gigs as influencers and advice-givers. For example, Mike Johnson, a Republican from Louisiana and the Speaker of the House at the time of this writing, is a Southern Baptist who hosts the podcast *Truth Be Told* with his wife Kelly, a pastoral counselor. In 2022, they released a two-part series on "Successful Parenting in a Culture Gone Awry" and several other parenting-related episodes, including "Protecting Our Kids from the Culture's Darkness." Nicholas Freitas, a Republican member of the Virginia House of Delegates, has built a large social media following (1.3 million followers on Instagram) and hosts a podcast, using both platforms to talk about conservative politics as well as his faith and his parenting philosophy.

Johnson and Freitas leverage their political platforms to reach an audience looking for Christian parenting advice. Halberstadt has built an audience through her motherhood and home-design content and from that speaks to her audience about politics. This road between the political and the parental (paved in part by Dobson) allows anyone with spiritual influence to take on the role of omnicompetent pastor or guide, giving advice on how followers should vote, discipline their kids, detox their kitchen, and educate their children. A post by one mid-level Christian mom influencer whose brand is "conservative homefront in the war on motherhood" illustrates this dynamic as she outlines the policy changes she is looking forward to in a Donald Trump presidency as an "ultra-crunchy, anti-vax, freebirthing, Christian, business owner, SAHM [stay-at-home mom]."[27]

Allie Beth Stuckey, a media influencer with over six hundred thousand followers on Instagram, has one foot in lifestyle content and the other in political activism. For her, as for Halberstadt, her politics lend credibility to her advice in other areas, and vice versa. Although Stuckey's primary focus isn't child-rearing, her lifestyle-influencer niche allows her to offer advice to the thousands of listeners to her *Relatable* podcast, with episodes like "When to Stop Having Kids," "The Dangers of Gentle Parenting," and "The Storybook Bibles Promoting Atheism to Kids." Stuckey hosts an annual Christian women's conference in Dallas called Share the Arrows (Halberstadt is a regularly featured speaker, alongside celebrity lifestyle influencers such as Candace Cameron Bure and conservative commentator Rosaria Butterfield), which promises "fellowship with likeminded women who are ready to Share the Arrows with you, armed with truth and courage in an age of deception and cowardice."[28]

Culture-war conservatism is easy to identify in the Christian parenting influencer sphere, where "biblical" has become both a claim about authority and a cultural identity, signaling social conservatism, a particular view of the Bible, and belonging to a particular Christian subculture. The use of Scripture baptizes the work of the Christian influencer, just as the term "biblical" baptized the advice of Tedd Tripp, James Dobson, and others who sought the same audience fifty years ago. But even though there is a lot of common ground between Christian parenting influencers and their predecessors, social media has changed what it means, and what it looks like, to be a good Christian parent.

A Parent-Focused Approach

Influencer culture is inherently individualistic and consumer-driven. In it, a persona is the ultimate marketing tool and proof-of-concept. Its financial apparatus depends on the creators' ability to capture our time and attention. In the parenting influencer space, the audience and focus of much online content is parents and *parental identity*. But the parent-centered nature of the influencer world and its content is distinct from what Ann Hulbert refers to as the "parent-centered" approach of James Dobson and his peers.[29] Popular Christian parenting teachers of the 1980s and '90s espoused an approach that underscored parental authority. Biblical parenting was defined by the rule of parents over the household rather than by the child-centered practices that defined attachment parenting, for example.[30]

Today's Christian parenting influencer content is parent-centered, but it focuses on the *experience* rather than the authority of parents. It shows consumers what being a parent looks like, feels like, and sounds like. Here, in audiovisual form, is how to respond with grace when our child does X. Here is how we fit in family devotionals every morning. Here is how we pray Scripture over our children. Here is how we prioritize romance in our marriage with a busy family of eight.

In some ways, the focus on the experience of Christian parenthood takes emphasis off child behavior and discipline, at least in public posts. Influencers may offer more advice in direct messages, in "ask me anything" series, or through downloadable ebooks and courses. There is still practical advice, but just as important as the advice itself is the aesthetic frame used to offer it. This new version of parent-centered advice found in the current parenting moment unavoidably idealizes Christian parenthood through beautiful aesthetics.

Christian influencers haven't entirely replaced the traditional market for Christian parenting books. Paul David Tripp's *Parenting* (2016) and Emily Jensen and Laura Wifler's *Risen Motherhood* (2019) both sold over one hundred thousand copies and remain popular resources. But it's worth noting that Jensen and Wifler built the audience for their book through social media, using platforms like Instagram and Facebook to attract Christian moms to an online community. The line between "author" and "influencer" in the Christian parenting world has become blurry, and Christian publishing rewards big platforms with book deals that heighten the credibility of people who are often giving parenting advice based on little else than personal experience.

The parent-centeredness of influencer content hasn't made it less political. Influencers have made parent-centeredness prettier and more winsome, though. Christian influencers on platforms like Instagram present gauzy, romantic images of countercultural homes in which husbands and wives play their parts, and children play theirs, all according to a biblical blueprint.

In that biblical blueprint, traditional gender roles are essential.

The Momfluencer Market

Most experts offering Christian parenting advice have traditionally been men. Even before the Christian parenting book boom, most people writing books for Christian families were male pastors, although we suspect that the people consuming these resources have predominately been women. The rise of Christian parenting influencers hasn't upended this traditional gender hierarchy, but it has subverted it in some ways.

Today, most Christian parenting influencers are mothers, and the gendered nature of influencer culture on platforms like Instagram has redistributed the power in the market for Christian parenting expertise. "Momfluencer" culture packages the often-invisible labor of motherhood as entertainment, or inspirational and educational content, such that moms can leverage their domestic roles and monetize their day-to-day lives.

"Instagram allows mothers to curate their own versions of motherhood, to pick and choose scenes they want to represent themselves, to edit the content according to their personal aesthetics and belief systems," writes Sara Petersen in her book, *Momfluenced*. "And why not? The actual labor of motherhood is private and rarely celebrated in any meaningful way. There's something empowering about mothers controlling their own narratives and imagery, when, for much of history, the story of motherhood was largely told (or wholly ignored) by men."[31]

Mothers tend to build some of the most expansive platforms in the parenting influencer ecosystem, both inside and outside Christian circles. And in the world of Christian parenting, influencer culture has allowed many women to take on "unofficial" but highly visible spiritual leadership roles. This is part of a pattern described by Kate Bowler in *The Preacher's Wife*. In a world that still effectively excludes women from the pulpit, the traditional power center in American evangelicalism, they have turned to the marketplace to lead and minister.[32] Male pastors or husband-wife teams authored many of the Christian parenting books of the 1980s and '90s, but as time went on, women began to write directly to other women, something that's only increased with momfluencers. For instance, Joel Osteen's Lakewood Church, at the time of this writing one of the largest megachurches in the United States, averages between 40,000 and 45,000 weekly attendees (Osteen published his book for mothers, *Your Best Life Now for Moms*, in 2007), but at the peak of their ministry, Risen Motherhood had an Instagram following of 324,000, about eight times larger than Osteen's congregation.[33] The comparison between a parenting resource and a church may seem ham-fisted, but when you consider the power of parasocial relationships cultivated on social media and through other outlets like podcasts and blogs, the online communities that coalesce around popular parenting influencers begin to resemble virtual congregations.

A close look at the bios and content of popular Christian parenting influencers shows that many of these creators are monetizing their platforms in novel ways. Without a following of fifty thousand or more, publishing a book with a major press might not be realistic, but books aren't the only marketable product for a parenting influencer. Affiliate links, Amazon storefronts, and sponsored content enable Christian momfluencers to market everything from collagen supplements to Bible-story board books to essential oils to devotional journals to "intimacy courses" with sex tips for married couples.

Christian influencer spaces mirror the uncomfortable realities of influencer culture. Many conventionally attractive, thin, White women have successfully leveraged their existing financial privilege to build a marketable, monetizable lifestyle.[34] "The medium is the message" becomes "The person is the message." The influencer and their ideas, worldview, politics, and advice are inseparable—all part of the same feed.

Even though conservative Christian women can exercise more spiritual and political authority in online spaces than they often are allowed in their own churches, gender roles and hierarchy are still crucial to the framework of good Christian parenting. Social media is a place where influencers can show rather than tell what it means to be a biblical woman, man, mother, or father, but whether they turn to online content or books, good Christian moms and dads have always been told that biblical manhood and womanhood are the prerequisites to good Christian parenthood.

Part 2

What Do We Find Here?

The Central Myths of Good Christian Parenting

3

UMBRELLAS OF AUTHORITY

A Blueprint for the Christian Family

Perhaps you have seen the "umbrellas of protection" illustration. Intended to model the so-called biblical principle of authority, this image includes several nesting umbrellas, each one smaller than the one before. Christ's umbrella, the biggest, covers a "pastor" umbrella, which covers a smaller "husband" umbrella, which covers a "wife" umbrella, which covers the children, who, in the original version, have no umbrella of their own.

According to this model, stepping outside the chain of command means stepping outside God's protective covering, leading to bad things. Every new parent has a moment when they realize their own powerlessness—buckling the car seat for the first time or running for a thermometer to check that first midnight fever or perhaps even earlier with heartbreaking news following a prenatal ultrasound. Parenthood forces us to reckon with how out of control life is, and Christian parenting tips that promise protection or control are incredibly appealing.

If you do it right, you and your child will be safe. It's a heady promise, especially for parents worried that their children may be lost to cultural drift or for adults who came from fractured and chaotic homes or for new parents navigating the day-in, day-out mundane responsibilities of adulthood.

The umbrella image is typically attributed to Bill Gothard, but multiple parenting resources use similar pictures. There's Tedd Tripp's "circle of safety," an illustration designed to show that obedient children secure promised good, and those who leave the circle are vulnerable to dangers. Doug Wilson's "generational faithfulness" idea promises devout parents that if they follow the correct blueprints, they can expect faithful future generations. These paradigms rest on two key elements common to evangelical family-life teaching: hierarchy and promised security.

In chapter 2, we discussed how Christian parenting experts of the 1960s and '70s urged a return to law and order and to obeying godly authorities. These beliefs came with a longing for a chain-of-command past, where, as Tripp explains, "there was a general concept of one's station in life and behaving in the manner appropriate to it." Tripp gives examples of a mom submitting to a dad, of a dad submitting to an employer, and of people submitting to state authorities. Then Tripp presents readers with an either/or decision: Either parents model submission to God-given hierarchies or their children will learn "unbiblical independence and rebellion." Tripp pits "various liberation movements" against the Bible: "Since our culture's interest in the equality and dignity of individuals is not rooted in Scripture," he explains, "we have lost the idea of respect for a person because of his or her office or place of authority."[1]

Many evangelicals believe that gender determines a person's rightful place in a God-ordained hierarchy. Certain paths are open to men that are not open to women and vice versa. Defending the distinctions between the two is viewed as a crucial marker of obedience to Scripture. The past fifty years have seen redoubled efforts by American evangelicals to bolster traditional gender norms against swift cultural changes around sex, gender, and the family unit. These efforts show up in parenting literature that teaches parents to fulfill their roles and raise children to follow suit.

The Pastor Umbrella Sets the Pattern

Many pastor-teachers connect ideas about hierarchy to Bible verses and take readers "back to the garden," looking to Genesis 1–2 for applications to modern family life, the idea being that teaching mothers and fathers how to have strong marriages will provide a secure homelife for children.

Gary and Anne Marie Ezzos' "Right Beginnings" chapter in *Growing Kids God's Way* exhorts parents to prevent children from disrupting the primacy of the marriage relationship. They recommend practices to counter what they call "child-centric parenting." The Ezzos are perhaps best known for their *Baby Wise* feeding schedules, intended to make sure newborns don't upset parental authority. They teach daily "couch time" as a marriage builder, where mom and dad sit on the couch wholly focused on each other within eyesight of the children, who are not to interrupt. "If children were necessary to complete man and woman," the Ezzos write, "God would have created them before [proclaiming that his creation was very good]."[2]

Evangelicals are often the first and loudest to claim that "children are a blessing," yet this messaging places children at the bottom of a set hierarchy, defined by obedience, submission, and relationship to a parent. In that framing, children are afterthoughts in the garden and accessories—arrows to fulfill a father's aims, olive shoots around a mother's table, non-player background characters who exist to rise up and bless their parents.

To be sure, parents who turn to these resources are often simply looking for parenting help or a Christian perspective on this new season of life. But these resources introduce them to archetypes in which *everyone* has a station and role to fill, something that adjacent Christian marriage resources reinforce. As a result, part of becoming a good Christian parent involves learning how to be a good Christian husband and a good Christian wife. In many evangelical churches, parish ministry presents marriage, motherhood, and fatherhood as *the* primary means for spiritual maturity, a relatively new dynamic given the scope of church history.

It's good for us to recall that the early church upheld the vocation of celibacy *alongside* the vocation of marriage and family. The third-century desert hermits devoted their solitary lives to fasting, prayer, and virginity. Some early leaders questioned whether sexual intercourse even within marriage was holy.[3] As time went on, devout Christians cloistered themselves behind abbey or monastery walls, away from worldly affairs such as marriage and childbirth, where they focused on prayer and good deeds.

The Protestant Reformation reclaimed the idea that ordinary Christians could also please God in the marketplace and family life. The Protestant image of the "holy household" and the Catholic picture of a "domestic monastery" influenced colonial America until the locus of economic activity shifted dramatically during the Industrial Revolution, and floods of people left their homes to work for a paycheck, purchasing goods made somewhere else and bringing them home to their families. This economic and domestic revolution set a different norm for American families such that today we can hardly conceive of self-contained communities, let alone self-sufficient households.

Over time, the pendulum in Protestant churches swung all the way, placing marriage and family on pedestals and treating chaste single people and childless couples as deficient. The focus on marriage and parenthood as the pinnacle of Christian adulthood has filled the evangelical market with resources telling singles how to prepare for marriage and married people how to organize their families in the godliest way.[4]

These resources on marriage and family include practical advice based on *ontological* arguments about what it means to be a godly man and a godly woman. They imply that it is inherently masculine for men to leave the house to provide and lead and inherently feminine for women to be submissive and manage the home. While many Christians throughout history would affirm that there are biological or God-designed differences between men and women, the late twentieth century's shifting norms around gender motivated American evangelicals to present people with the "correct," Christian way to fulfill these gender roles.

The Birth of Complementarian Teaching

In 1991, as a response to the perceived growing influence of feminism in the evangelical movement, a group of theologians and pastors argued for a "biblical vision of sexual complementarity"[5] and published *Recovering Biblical Manhood and Womanhood*. This movement-defining book argues that there is a biblically prescribed manhood and womanhood and that this distinction has been lost. The authors disagree with interpretations that understand patriarchy to be a result of the fall and instead accept gender hierarchy as a part of God's created order.[6]

Here, complementarian ideas are offered to secure God's best for evangelical marriages. These teachings align with mainstream images of men as the heads of the home and the kings of the castle. Christian fathers are to be strong protectors, responsible for all those who fall under their headship. "It would be unnatural," pastor John Piper explains, "in the normal family setting for the husband/father to . . . surrender the task of 'breadwinning' to his wife."[7] Fathers are also to be spiritual leaders, taking on what Elisabeth Elliot and Tim and Beverly LaHaye call a priestly role within the home. Dobson tells men that if a family exceeds its budget, neglects Bible study and church, or has disrespectful children, "the primary responsibility lies with the father."[8]

One of the respondents to our informal survey of adults who grew up in households that subscribed to these teachings describes how the pressure on fathers to perform came with heavy doses of shame and an impossible standard of perfection:

> The most harmful thing, and at the time I didn't know this because I thought it was my responsibility, but the concept that I held ultimate responsibility for the spiritual wellness of the whole house was such a burden. . . . Now, in hindsight, I think it buries men, because you can't possibly live up to that. Your kids are their own persons, and so is your partner. But under that umbrella, they can't be. They have to be extensions of you.
>
> —Justin[9]

Fathers are to be present and active at home while also being the sole provider. They need to make enough money to sustain a single-income household while not being too invested in their careers. Headship means being the spiritual leader too, which involves church and devotional activities. Men, regardless of personality, background, or interests, are to achieve these standards of masculinity and encourage their sons and mentees, the future leaders of churches and families, to do the same. We see this in the gender-specific parenting books that began appearing at the turn of the twenty-first century.

Boys to Men

James Dobson's popular book *Bringing Up Boys* (2001) was one of the first gender-specific resources published in the late '90s and early '00s.[10] Dobson addresses everything from absent fathers to unisex toy marketing to sexual orientation to boy-specific education and discipline, alongside many other cultural concerns of the moment. Dobson's books were some of the few in the evangelical market that attempted to discuss contemporary psychological and child-development research. This stands in marked contrast to the Bible-alone resources of his nouthetic counseling peers. While Dobson's select inclusion of research might have brought benefits, particularly compared with other resources that viewed all external expertise with suspicion, it also lent an unexamined credibility to his claims about sex and gender.

Changing American attitudes regarding sexual identity and gender had evangelicals pushing back against anything that would "confuse" roles that were associated with boyhood and girlhood. Dobson recommended that parents of "effeminate boys or masculinized girls" scrutinize their own practices as mothers and fathers, because "growing up straight isn't something that happens. It requires good parenting."[11] So fathers of sons who "appear effeminate, gender-confused, or chronically uncomfortable with same sex peers"[12] are told to seek out "reparative therapy," to engage their sons in "rough-and-tumble games," to have them hammer pegs into a pegboard, or to "take [their son] into the shower, where the boy cannot help but notice that Dad has a penis just like his, only bigger."[13]

Other pastor-teachers offered opinions without any attempt to account for cultural context or change across time and history. Boys were described with mythical, cinematic appeal, and the inclusion of Bible verses elevated these archetypes to word-of-God truth. For instance, Douglas Wilson's *Future Men: Raising Boys to Fight Giants* opens with summary categories that he uses to define "the shape of masculinity"—lords, husbandmen, saviors, sages, and glory-bearers.[14]

Entire subcultures developed around idealized masculinity. Vision Forum, an organization started by homeschooling leader Douglas Phillips, held father-son retreats and annual conferences where families could reenact moments of masculine valor like the *Titanic*'s "women and children first" call to self-sacrifice or WWII vets storming Normandy's beaches. Parents could purchase toys like lassos, bows and arrows, swords, and survival gear to help their sons grow in godly boyhood from the "All-American Boys Adventure Catalog." (Girls could browse dolls, dresses, parasols, and play kitchens from "The Beautiful Girlhood Collection.")[15] Godly boyhood took whatever shape the preferences of the community prescribed; for Gothard's followers, boys needed to be clean-shaven, dressed in button-downs, preparing for apprenticeships and courtship. Such markers could reassure parents their sons wouldn't be lost to the surrounding culture of effeminacy.

Wilson tells parents that a boy's "natural" response to effeminacy should be *yuck* and that "for those boys who gravitate toward playing house, and dolls, and dress-ups, wise parental control, oversight, and redirection is necessary."[16] There was no room for boys who fell outside the mold, especially as American evangelicals reacted to the LGBTQ+ movement and new conversations about sexual identity. It became even more important for Christian parents to get gender *right* in their families, and this goal left children whose interests failed to conform, regardless of sexual orientation, further alienated.

Fathers needed to reclaim and model masculinity, something that shape-shifted according to the cultural appetites of the moment. John Eldredge, who wrote the best-selling book *Wild at Heart*, calls American men out of what he describes as a passive effeminate piety and into adventurous masculinity. Eldredge compares his vision of a Braveheart-esque Christian warrior with the unwelcome niceness of Mr. Rogers: "[Rogers] is simply a good picture of Christianity reduced to being nice. That would not get a man crucified. That isn't the picture of

Christ or of his man. If Rogers were our dad, we would carry wounds of passivity."[17]

For Eldredge, masculinity is active, questing, and aligned with his own personal interests as an outdoorsman. His tone is more winsome than similar messaging that comes from harsher social critics such as Mark Driscoll, who faulted contemporary Christianity for presenting Jesus as a "Richard Simmons, hippie, queer Christ," a "neutered and limp-wristed popular Sky Fairy of pop culture."[18] For both Eldredge and Driscoll, a defining feature of correct Christian masculinity tells us what it is not: weak, passive, and feminine. The synonymous nature of these pejorative descriptors reveals latent misogyny as well as an either/or vision of externally applied, insider-defined masculinity. This vision of a tough Jesus excludes someone like Fred Rogers, whose work, by contrast, aims to help boys and girls achieve internal social and emotional intelligence. Boys, men, and teenagers who don't fit the manly-man aesthetics of achievement, success, and conquest are sidelined as "nice," irrelevant, and failing to measure up as men.

This impossible quest continues to the present day, where the "red-pilled" manosphere influencers of the 2020s assign the moniker "biblical" to abstract concepts of headship and leadership and define them to include weightlifting, whiskey drinking, hustle culture, and any number of subjective markers.

This is all a lot for men—and boys—to shoulder, and the biblical blueprint requires women and girls to help alleviate the strain. Elizabeth George, a writer of popular books for women, advises, "Countries with monarchs fly the royal flag over the palace when the king is in residence, and the hurry and scurry of servants' feet can be heard throughout the castle during his stay. Adopting this attitude and this approach (have your kids join you!) will help you pamper and love your king when he arrives home."[19]

Call in the helpmeets.

A Woman's Place Is in the Home

The original umbrella image labels the wife umbrella "children managers of the home." It's a revealing (and ungrammatical) word choice. Traditional gender norms in the church teach women to focus on the home. Evangelical resources for mothers dial in on this, presenting a picture of mythical motherhood that draws on Victorian ideals of hearth and home that have long captivated the American imagination.[20] Evangelical mothers are to focus on building a "castle," a refuge from the world for their husbands—first and foremost—and their children.

Books marketed to Christian mothers invariably include homemaking tips and relationship advice alongside spiritual instruction. Early on, popular female authors like Edith Schaeffer taught readers how to beautify their homes, prepare meals, and fine-tune their hosting skills as a form of evangelistic outreach and the ideal way to raise children. According to Dorothy Patterson, a contributor to *Recovering Biblical Manhood and Womanhood*, "Keeping the home is God's assignment to the wife—even down to changing the sheets, doing the laundry, and scrubbing the floors."[21] Countless other authors held up the Proverbs 31 woman as an example of suburban domesticity; women were taught to translate their business acumen, creative pursuits, and wise investments into household management.

This kind of teaching made the division of household labor a question of eternal significance. It also pressured many evangelical women navigating the "mommy wars" of the 1970s and '80s to become stay-at-home moms. Christian women who worked outside the home risked disastrous consequences. Patterson warned about "an increase in strident lesbianism and open homosexuality, a quantum upward leap in divorces, an increase in rapes and sexual crimes of all sorts—and families smaller in size than ever before" should women choose to work outside the home. "While I am not implying that every career woman is selfish, I am saying that the social atmosphere that causes women to crave professional pursuits over the family is perverted by unbiblical assumptions and an ungodly spirit of assertion and self-gratification."[22] In 1985, Mary Pride published *The Way Home*, the first of many anti-feminist books that presented stay-at-home motherhood as "biblical," without consideration of the way domestic arrangements have varied across time and culture or how opting out of the marketplace is a choice available only to privileged families.[23]

It is impossible to overstate how much Christian family resources emphasized homemaking for women. A mother's domain could include things like authoring books, creating homeschool resources to sell, or participating in home-based businesses, such as multilevel marketing. This permissible supplementary income could be a lifeline for families struggling to make a father's single income work (though a mother's paid work could not displace a father's role as provider or interfere with her domestic and child-rearing work). Mothers who had the resources to pursue traditional homesteading arts—sewing, milling flour, baking sourdough bread, canning and preserving—embodied godly femininity. For instance, Pearl Barrett and Serene Allison created Trim Healthy Mama, a multimedia empire to help mothers learn biblical principles for nutrition while maintaining a desirable female form. Influencer Rebekah Merkle recently launched a home decor streaming series so that followers can learn how to glorify God with their furniture arrangement.[24]

Of course, none of these pursuits are bad or fabricated. But telling Christian women they are part of a God-designed blueprint in which only certain activities are deemed worthy or acceptable extends far beyond any semblance of biblical support for it. And when ideas about domesticity combine with ideas about complementarian roles, Christian wives and mothers are told to tailor these preapproved activities *in order to* please their husbands.

A Woman's Work Is Never Done

Writing in the late '90s, Elizabeth George accidentally reveals how deference to a husband's authority shifts into the realm of idolatry when she recounts how a woman named Sue came to her for advice about a potential job. George asked what her husband thought about it. "[Sue] quickly answered, 'Oh, he doesn't want me to do it.' 'Why, Sue,' I exclaimed, 'God has spoken!'"[25] It is clear in the book that George means God has spoken *through* the biblical blueprint for submission, but the phrasing is revealing. George interprets the creation order she perceives in Genesis 2:18 to be a flattening simplification: "I was to serve Jim."[26]

She encourages mothers to similarly plan their days around this goal:

- "Help your husband."
- "Focus on your husband."
- Ask yourself: "Will this help or hinder my husband?"
- "Choose your husband over all other human relationships."
- Ask yourself: "Am I spoiling my husband rotten?"
- "Pray for him daily."
- "Plan for him daily."
- "Prepare for him daily."
- "Please him."
- "Protect your time with him."
- "Physically love him."
- "Positively respond to him."
- "Praise him."[27]

Embracing motherhood with excellence, then, means preemptively thinking of ways to serve one's husband and children, but also taking care lest one's husband and children become idols. Christina Fox, an author and counselor who writes for outlets like the Gospel Coalition, authored a book to help mothers recognize their idols. "You could say I worshiped sleep," Fox writes.[28] She explains how the early newborn days had her thinking about sleep all the time, and she encourages women to focus on God's sufficiency instead. Fox applies this lesson to the physical and emotional challenges of every stage of motherhood, including the empty nest. "If my children give my life purpose and meaning, if they are idols in my heart, I will find myself in despair once they are gone. I will feel lost and unanchored."[29] This is the Christian mother's double bind: She must adopt an identity entirely absorbed by wifehood and motherhood, but if she grieves a difficult marriage, infertility, or an empty nest, she is condemned for wanting too much or loving too much.

Being a keeper at home involves a tidy kept-in-order house and a tidy under-control soul, with undesirable emotions acting as indicators of sin or misguided priorities. Nancy Leigh DeMoss says as much, conjuring the umbrellas image: "When we place ourselves under the spiritual covering of the authorities God has placed in our lives, God protects us." She goes on to explain how submission is "liberating" and that if women don't find it so, it's possible they are experiencing satanic attack or have a problem with authority.[30] Many resources notably include suggestions for coping with anxiety, depression, or unwanted feelings.[31] Elisabeth Elliot explains that "an ordered home means not only an acceptance of God's arrangement of authority, and a conscientious regard for time, but also making sure that there is a place for everything. If there isn't, it probably means there are too many things."[32] This represents the evangelical mother's task in a very literal sense but also a metaphorical one: Mothers must adapt to the blueprint, ridding themselves of anything—including personal interests, ambitions, or desires—that competes with biblical motherhood.

This is reinforced through storytelling and historical revisionism. Janette Oke, Francine Rivers, Beverly Lewis, and other fiction writers use their remarkable storytelling skills to create compelling novels with characters who embody the ideals of evangelical womanhood. Women from church history are pedestaled as examples of complementarian housewives and mothers. For instance, motherhood books sometimes recycle this apocryphal anecdote describing John Wesley's mother: "As a signal to her children to be quiet, Susanna would sometimes sit down and pull her apron over her head so that she could pray in peace. When she was thus accoutered, the children knew not to interrupt her."[33] These books present Susanna Wesley—who taught her children before the age of one to "fear the rod and cry softly" so "that most odious noise of the crying of children was rarely heard in the house"[34]—as a harried housewife who needed to hide from the chaos. This rendering manipulates history to support the mythology. In reality, Susanna was married to a negligent pastor husband and carried out ruthlessly exacting disciplinary methods that allowed her to maintain order.

The family tree of Jonathan and Sarah Edwards also features prominently in evangelical parenting resources—with lists of descendant doctors, lawyers, and professors serving as testimony to the generational blessing of following a godly blueprint.[35] Like Susanna, Sarah is presented as a paragon of suburban domesticity, with no mention of her historical realities—eleven children, an absent husband, and a colonial household subsidized by servants and the labor of enslaved people.[36] Susanna's and Sarah's lives are proof texted to motivate evangelical moms to achieve a mythical kind of excellent motherhood, regardless of the kind of partner they have.

Many issues of *Above Rubies*, a magazine for Christian mothers, include testimonies from women whose prayers were answered when their husbands finally became the spiritual leader in the home. It would be interesting to survey how many men entered their marriages viewing their wives this way and how many were led there—ironically—by their wives. What if a husband wants his wife to work outside the home? Enroll their children in "government" public schools? Attend a different church? Does a mother buck his authority, or does she submit and compromise the blueprint?

The authors of these books and articles attempt to answer such questions, offering pastoral guidance to readers whose circumstances vary widely. A mother whose husband is failing to provide might be encouraged to pray and trust God to provide rather than be empowered to get a job and help support the family. If a husband wants the children homeschooled, mothers who are drowning after back-to-back pregnancies may be told to try harder and cope. Women in dangerous situations may be told to remain and trust God to give them the grace to endure. The presumption that all men in Christian spaces are benevolent and gentle is stunningly out of touch with reported domestic abuse, let alone all that goes unreported.[37]

In the wake of the #MeToo movement, some Christian wives and mothers have told their stories publicly, recounting ways that biblical womanhood teaching enabled and cultivated abuse.[38] This should invite Christians to examine the fruit of such teachings, particularly because they are often passed down to the next generation—including our daughters.

A Girl's Place Is Also in the Home

Pick up any resource on evangelical girlhood, and you will find the counterpart to cinematic boyhood—princess tropes, ideas about beauty and being pursued by a man, and attempts to address "female shortcomings" such as gossip or jealousy. Additionally, girls raised in conservative evangelical homes are taught to fear and reject feminism. For instance, Bruce Wilkinson's popular video course *Biblical Portrait of a Marriage* includes fictional vignettes in which a preteen girl is mentored by women in her extended family. Aunt Lilith, a bitter, divorced, angry woman, is the only female character who resists what these videos prescribe as the Bible's teachings on womanhood. This powerfully depicts the way biblical womanhood messaging is passed on to Christian girls. Many women told us that as a rite of passage into adulthood, they were given resources like Martha Peace's *The Excellent Wife* or Debi Pearl's *Created to Be His Helpmeet* under the assumption that they would accept this blueprint without question.

A girl's apprenticeship begins early and in earnest, with daily opportunities to practice submission and service in the domestic sphere, something that contributes much-needed help to overwhelmed families with many children. Furthermore, if a woman's *primary* role is to complement and help a man, then it follows that a girl's *primary* role is to do the same, something that raises questions about education. If a woman's highest calling is to wifehood and motherhood, does she really need to go to college? Learn math beyond a junior-high level? Wouldn't it be better for her to learn how to run a household? The stay-at-home-daughter movement of the '90s and '00s said "absolutely," rejecting women's college education and encouraging girls to remain under their father's headship until they could be courted and wedded to a husband. And in single-income, home-educating families, the labor of parentified older children—most often, sisters—subsidizes the ideological lifestyle choices of their parents.

While many mainstream evangelical families don't go to such extremes, they dabble in lite versions of this thinking. Tween and teen girls are expected to look after younger children at group gatherings. Adults compliment girls on their domestic skills, appearance, or marriage prospects. Christian colleges joke about MRS degrees or earning "a ring by spring," implying that the adult ideal for Christian girls is marriage and, ultimately, motherhood.

In some evangelical circles, the father-daughter relationship is foregrounded with troubling messaging. James Dobson normalizes the idea that fathers will be involuntarily sexually attracted to their young adult daughters (and encourages dads to continue to offer hugs and physical contact despite this).[39] Things like purity rings and father-daughter balls reinforce the notion that a daughter's sexuality belongs to the men in her life—first her father, then her betrothed. Voddie Baucham, a pastor, author, and seminary president who endorsed the stay-at-home-daughter movement, unintentionally names the danger of sexualizing daughters in this way: "A lot of men are leaving their wives for younger women because they yearn for attention from younger women. And God gave them a daughter who can give them that."[40]

Such ideas leave girls vulnerable to abuse and prevent them from identifying their interests and desires, let alone planning for their future. Girls, robbed of education and needed skills that could allow them to provide for themselves, instead prepare to be completely dependent on a theoretical future husband. In situations where husbands turn out to be abusive, women and children are trapped without recourse.

Idolizing marriage, defining a woman as a helpmeet, and equating femininity with self-denial and servanthood all leave Christian girls and women ill-equipped for independent adult life and instead teach them to anticipate codependent relationships. When these ideas come wrapped up in cultural imagery and spiritual language, they can be very difficult to untangle. Challenging the mythology requires girls and women to step out from under the umbrellas of protection, indeed, to challenge the men in leadership tiers above them, something not allowed within many evangelical communities.[41]

Filling the Quiver

Some self-proclaimed parenting experts like Bill Gothard and Tedd Tripp warned parents about what might happen if they or their children stepped outside the hierarchy, while others like Doug Wilson and Doug Phillips enticed them with promises about generational legacy. "Children are a heritage from the LORD," so Psalm 127:3 goes, and the metaphor of children as arrows in the hands of their parents loomed large in the evangelical imagination. "Blessed is the man whose quiver is full of them" (v. 5).

Parenting books focus primarily on the child-rearing years, but some include directives about childbearing, married sexual activity, and contraception.[42] Because the biblical blueprint is based on ontological arguments, much is made of how procreation encapsulates the ideology—the generating leadership and initiation of the masculine meets the receptive surrender of the feminine.[43] This metaphor is extended to dating, where young men pursue and court virginal women who are waiting for "the one," early marriage is presented as ideal, and, since "true love waits," Christians can expect a blissful married sex life. Promises regarding the latter became staples of abstinence seminars where evangelical young people made commitments about theoretical sexual behavior and things like "welcoming as many children as God sends us," the implications of which they could not consider in a meaningful way.

Joshua Harris wrote the iconic evangelical courtship manual *I Kissed Dating Goodbye* (1997) when he was twenty-one. His friend Sam Torode wrote the preface, explaining how he fell in love with his future wife, Bethany Patchin, after reading her Focus on the Family article about saving the first kiss for marriage. Sam and Bethany later went on to pen the book *Open Embrace* (2002) as newlyweds. The Torodes posited a quiet theological case for evangelicals to forgo contraception, thereby demonstrating their trust in God's sovereignty.[44] Because if children are a blessing from the Lord, the logic follows that more children are more of a blessing.

Harris and the Torodes (all of whom are now divorced) later asked their publishers to discontinue their books, apologizing for the message they—as very young adults—had been platformed by their elders to dispense along ideological lines.[45] But versions of that message are alive and well in evangelical communities. As the culture wars of the late twentieth century intensified, children were increasingly seen as "arrows in the hand of a warrior" (Ps. 127:4). Quiverfull—the theological movement that suggests Christian couples should have as many children as possible—became popular as a vision of Western cultural dominance. Couples who don't or can't have biological children, mothers who haven't given birth, and families that fall outside the two-parent nuclear family mold are incidentally erased from this vision of blessing.[46] Large families are viewed as a sign of God's favor as well as a means by which to reform society. The Quiverfull movement goes hand in hand with Dominionism, a theology that envisions men "taking dominion" in their families and reforming American society into a theocratic Christian nation by outpopulating others. Quiverfull and Dominionist teaching is full of promises about a generational line that will impact the nation for centuries to come, a perspective that cannot conceive of children as persons all their own, who may grow up and choose a different path. But in the heady years when children are young, parents are drawn to these movements, adding "Christian nation building" to their biblical checklist. These subcultures were popular during the American homeschooling movements of the '90s and '00s, and we see a resurgence in their modern-day counterparts of tradwife culture and Christian nationalism.

The advice of Dobson, with his encouraging words for fathers tired out after working a nine-to-five job, seems quaint and "soft" compared with the rhetoric of today's Christian nationalism proponents. Josh Webbon, a pastor-influencer, recommends that a husband control his wife's reading and listening materials so she won't "outpace" him. Webbon describes a type of father who exerts absolute control over family life: "I have four people in my life that I dictate the hours in their day. I dictate what time they go to the bathroom. When we eat, what we eat, what we wear. They are my children. Those are the people that I have almost limitless authority with."[47]

Some evangelicals might see this as an overreach, but on what grounds? If a husband is the biblical God-ordained umbrella of protection, why shouldn't he determine what his wife reads? And if it is his wife's God-given duty to submit, complaining about it is a sin. Martha Peace, the preeminent female biblical counselor and author of *The Excellent Wife* and *The Faithful Parent*, supports this idea of male lordship, including "put off" charts for Christian wives. She tells wives to stop being irritated at their husband, to plan for the emotional turbulence around their period, to set aside designs on a job outside the home. Women are to "put off" the desire to have their needs met, to surrender their longing to be treated well, to trust God that if they feel they "can't take the pressure anymore . . . [they] can bear up under the pressure for as long as God deems necessary."[48]

We heard from many men and women who had been admonished to suffer for righteousness' sake under the crushing weight of these legalistic teachings. Perhaps the fact that Christian resources preemptively tell men and women how to deal with depression, anxiety, loneliness, fear, and sorrow reveals that the blueprint bears troubling fruit. As we see again and again, though, if the prescribed methods don't "work" for families, the problem is *them*—their inability to cope, to submit, to obey, to choose joy. This line of thinking keeps parents reaching for the next best-selling resource that promises a workable solution, a modern-day version of an apron over the head and a whispered prayer from overwhelmed mothers and fathers.

And what about the children? The children in the umbrella diagram have no umbrella of their own, not even a comma to separate them from their mother's task list: "children managers of the home." Many evangelical parents dutifully worked hard to shape family life according to hierarchies that presented children as nonpersons, responsibilities to be put in order alongside providing for and keeping the home. When a parent believes that their children are arrows meant for them to aim, when fathers and mothers believe that there are archetypes for biblical boyhood and girlhood, when Christians believe that God will send calamity if they step out from under the umbrellas of protection, what happens when a child takes a different path?

Evangelical frameworks generally don't address the process of children separating from their parents, something known as "differentiation" or "individuation." The expectation instead is that proper Christian parenting will produce children who fold into the frameworks taught them by their parents, who in turn believe these messages to be timeless, applicable biblical truths.

For a time, this may appear to be the case. In our survey, many adult children told us that the process of separating from or even disagreeing with their parents was delayed well into adulthood. Sometimes it took moving away from home, getting married, or the failure of things like the courtship ideal for a young adult to question the frameworks.

As teenagers, stay-at-home daughters Anna Sofia and Elizabeth Botkin mentored thousands of other girls through their blog, published books, and as featured speakers at conferences. They both remained unmarried until their late thirties. Their writing and speaking slowed as they quietly began working or chose paths at odds with the message they had for years offered to other young women.

We heard from many adults navigating this dissonance between the myths they had been taught and their lived reality. They are now deconstructing things like purity culture, gender roles, and other culturally specific beliefs that had become enmeshed with Christianity. We heard from people who still struggle to trust God's goodness in hardship, because they believe suffering to be a sign they have disobeyed and are outside his protection. Questioning these beliefs sometimes led to strained relationships or inauthentic connection with parents who didn't understand why their children were backsliding or rejecting God's plan. Parents perpetuated the myths, something that caused harm in the moment and also displaced the opportunity—year in and year out—for them to learn how to connect with their children as individuals. This left families uniquely ill-equipped for the moments when the blueprints failed them and the myths were exposed.

Adults raised under these teachings are leaving the church at record rates. What reasons do they give? Young women exiting en masse cite sexism as a major reason, and 60 percent of adults leaving their childhood religion identify "negative treatment of gay and lesbian people" as a motivating factor.[49] Anxious parents may have found it reassuring to box their young children in with ideas about biblical manhood and womanhood, but as children grow, there may come a time when the box bursts. And if the box is so tightly wrapped up with teaching about divinely ordained authority and protection, it also frays ideas about the goodness of God and the trustworthiness of orthodox Christian teaching. When timebound cultural perspectives are presented as timeless truths, people who come to recognize and reject the former may have difficulty retaining any of the latter. Indeed, the entire contemporary movement of deconstruction is a direct response to ways evangelical teaching shaped a generation.

Today, if you look for Gothard's umbrella image online, you will likely find one of two kinds of posts. There will be adults pointing out the flaws, naming the way this teaching harmed them, perhaps navigating the fallout with wry humor. You will also find sincere Christian parents sharing the image as instructive, commenting that "God's ways are best," and perpetuating the same old myths for a new generation of families.

4

WHO'S IN CHARGE HERE?

The Testimony of Well-Behaved Children

My (Kelsey's) kids like to run. A lot. A giant open room is an invitation to fly from one end to the other, squealing and giggling as they go. On a Sunday last summer, between services at our church, my kids were running around the auditorium. Admittedly, I could have put a stop to it sooner, but there was nothing going on in the room, and it was mostly empty. I chose, that morning, to let the play continue and didn't think much of it.

When it was time to head out the door, I started to walk across the room to catch the attention of my oldest, and I heard a quiet voice remark (I think good-naturedly, but who knows), "Looks like someone's lost control there."

I chuckled to myself and thought, *Lost control? When did I ever* have *control?*

Many parents can relate to that feeling or to hearing someone say under their breath, "I would never let my kid do that!" or "I can't believe she's letting them act like this."

"Let." "Allow." "Lose control." This way of talking about the relationship between parent and child, particularly in public spaces, is common. It's something every parent feels on a regular basis: Other adults expect them to be able to control their children, and parents will be judged based on their ability to do so. If a parent *can't* do so, they may win back some favor by being sufficiently stern and demonstrating that they take their child's behavior *very* seriously. An apology to onlookers wouldn't hurt, either.

In many Christian communities, docile, obedient children are evidence of a firmly established authority structure in the home. "Good behavior" is a signpost of a child's bright future, and bad behavior ultimately is traced back to the parents. As a result, the inability to control, rein in, or command one's children is seen as a moral failure.

James Dobson, Tedd Tripp, Larry Christenson, Gary and Anne Marie Ezzo, Chuck Swindoll, Bill Gothard, Elisabeth Elliot, and other evangelical pastor-teachers write about the importance of the authority structure of the family. It is to be passionately practiced and defended, and if children are "allowed" to stray from parental authority, all of society will eventually collapse into lawless anarchy. But every honest parent will admit that they simply *don't* have absolute control over their children. And in many cases, the extent to which they can "control" a child is only the extent to which they are able and willing to physically restrain or overpower a child. So what are we really talking about when we say that a parent has "lost control"?

Christian parenting experts express differing views about the level of control or influence parents should expect to have over their children. However, they all zero in on particular behaviors and, perhaps more importantly, what particular behaviors mean. Good or bad behaviors have spiritual, social, and political implications. For many evangelical pastor-teachers, obedience to parents is obedience to God. Children don't need any tools to distinguish between the two, and they will learn to walk with God only by learning to follow parental instruction.

Some experts are more practical about obedience, offering some version of the common advice that "if you train for obedience, you won't have to train for anything else."[1] James Dobson, Tim Kimmel (executive director of Grace Based Families and author of multiple parenting books), and Chuck Swindoll write as though the future of America depends on parents' ability to produce obedient, well-behaved children. Dobson writes, "Nothing short of a great Civil War of Values rages today throughout North America. Two sides with vastly differing and incompatible world-views are locked in a bitter conflict that permeates every level of society. . . . Children are the prize to the winners of the second great Civil War."[2]

Discipline and behavior modification are a social and political project as well as a spiritual one. These authors often start with a social problem plaguing society (usually having to do with adolescent or young-adult behavior) and work backward, lamenting that if only Christian parents had the right advice, tools, and determination, they could have prevented . . . (fill in the blank).

The aesthetics of a mythical family life build the platforms and brands of Christian parenting influencers. On social media, style, physical attractiveness, and wealth do the heavy lifting when it comes to capturing an audience. But for parenting influencers, the ways children conduct themselves on camera are part of the imagined ideal they are projecting. When influencers feature their children as part of their platform, behavior becomes part of the fantasy. In Christian content and media, behavior also becomes part of the family's testimony.

Who's Going to Pay for This?

The perception of child behavior as evidence of a parent's or family's goodness is not new. Parents have always been blamed for their children's mistakes and often have no choice but to absorb the consequences or costs associated with them. If a toddler trips over a cord and breaks a lamp, the parent pays to replace it—at least, that's the expectation.

In public, people tend to blame parents for their children's behavior when it suits them, when their annoyance needs something or someone to land on. If a child screams at a restaurant, onlookers wonder, *Why are those parents letting their child behave like this?* And there is almost always disagreement about what it looks like to hold parents accountable for a child's behavior. Failure to judge correctly and act accordingly may come with painful social consequences for the whole family.

Today, social media is a common platform for publicly shaming parents. TikTok features endless clips of parents struggling in public with their children, often posted by people offering cynical commentary or a series of judgy facial expressions. There are videos of children yelling at their parents or throwing tantrums, taken without permission and offered on the internet for litigation. Spectators in the comment section act as the jury: Is this a failure of a permissive, pushover parent? Is this just a normal (but very hard) episode? Does the mom look tired? Has this kid had too much Red Dye 40?

Dobson relies on a kind of public shaming of parents in his books, which include many anecdotes about tyrannical toddlers dominating their hapless parents and horror stories about delinquent adolescents who were not properly disciplined when they were young enough to learn respect for authority. In the opening to *The Strong-Willed Child* (1985), Dobson recalls watching a mother help her children board a bus in Los Angeles. He describes the children as "rambunctious" and a "wiggling tribe" and the mother as noticeably disheveled: "Her hair was a mess and the gaunt look on her face revealed a state of utter exhaustion."[3]

While perhaps Dobson meant this story as a comfort to parents who were also in a state of "utter exhaustion," his observations throughout the book make one thing abundantly clear: Parents and their children are being watched. A reader might well finish his book with the impression that if they ever visited Dobson's neighborhood, they'd better leave the kids at home. Some parenting expert might catch you looking tired, or, worse, they might catch you parenting rambunctious children.

The judgment coming from Christian parenting experts carries a unique weight because it is infused with eternal stakes. When Dobson describes a strong-willed child, he does not neutrally describe difficult behaviors. He makes claims about a child's sin nature and how it should be dealt with: "Perhaps this tendency toward self-will is the essence of 'original sin' which has infiltrated the human family. It certainly explains why I place such stress on the proper response to willful defiance during childhood, for that rebellion can plant the seeds of personal disaster."[4] The "perhaps" at the beginning of this passage suggests the claim that follows is just a hunch, but does that really soften it at all? Most of the "perhaps-es" and "in-my-opinions" in a book like *The Strong-Willed Child* precede claims and diagnoses offered with authority and finality. After all, this is advice coming from *Dr. James Dobson*. Isn't he the expert on God's design and will for the family?

Good Behavior as Holy Order

As we discussed in chapter 2, it is impossible to separate popular Christian parenting books of the late twentieth century from the aims of the Christian Right. Family values were a key tenet of that agenda—as was law and order. Nixon's ability to rally voters around the cause of restoring order was arguably what secured his 1968 election. Historian Michael Flamm observes that liberals failed to articulate a strategy to address growing panic over crime and unrest, whereas conservatives managed to speak with a more "cogent moral voice" on issues related to law enforcement, something the American public was desperately seeking.[5] That cogent moral voice from conservatives fueled the Christian Right's ascendance during the 1970s and helped propel Dobson to fame. Nixon martialed a stern, authoritative voice and message. Dobson did the same as he delivered his ideas about the importance of discipline. The word "discipline" had appeared in the titles of Christian parenting literature before, but *Dare to Discipline* and the timing of its publication met the moment.

One of our survey respondents grew up in a home where her parents relied on child-rearing advice from Dobson and Tedd Tripp. She told us that keeping children "in line" was of the utmost importance in her home and faith community. Adults' authority was to be respected without question, even when it came to their beliefs about a child's intent or inner thoughts.

> Motivations were assumed and ascribed by those in authority. And if an authority ascribed a motive to something you did, you accepted their judgment as being right since you thought yourself incapable of truly knowing your own motives and would never argue with an adult.
>
> —Rachel

One major point of divergence between popular Christian parenting books and mainstream literature is the labeling of particular behaviors as "sin." Whereas child psychologists and secular parenting influencers might use a term like "developmentally appropriate" to describe a toddler's emphatic *No!*, many Christian parenting experts label such behavior as rooted in sin nature or as willful rebellion.

Many of the individuals we surveyed recalled that, in their homes, disobedience was broadly defined in a way that could include both open defiance and childish silliness. Some look back and wonder if the behaviors that were punished most aggressively were those that were simply unpleasant to their parents rather than measured by some objective standard of right and wrong.

Lauren, who grew up in a fundamentalist Baptist community, said that her parents' view of child behavior came from Gary and Anne Marie Ezzo. Spanking with either a hand or an object like a wooden spoon was practiced regularly:

> Disobedience was defined as anything that didn't align with my parents, my mother in particular. It could be anything from perceived attitude, emotion that was unwelcome, or a chore that was done too quickly or not quickly enough. The definition was malleable and based on the mood of my mother more than anything else. It was always a sin to do anything that displeased the person with authority.

When parents believe that children's good behavior means their family is adhering to God's divine order, they may start seeing pet peeves, disruptiveness, assertions of differing opinions, or even mildly annoying shenanigans as an affront to their authority. Expectations for obedience become all encompassing. It's not enough that a child obeys; they must obey with a happy heart. To illustrate what it looks like to require cheerful compliance, author and pastor Douglas Wilson recounts an interaction between his daughter, Rachel (the author of her own parenting book, *Loving the Little Years*), and her daughter (his granddaughter): Rachel told her daughter, "'Blaire, I said no, so you have to control your heart. Show me how you control your heart. What do you do?' Blaire stopped and said, 'Smile.'"[6]

In *The Strong-Willed Child*, Dobson simultaneously offers grace, "*Nothing* will make an eighteen-month-old child act like a five-year-old,"[7] but also instructs parents how to properly spank a child of that age.[8] Dobson acknowledges that nothing can make a child accelerate through the already-rapid mental and physical changes they are experiencing, but, he insists, making them act more mature isn't the point. The point of spanking a toddler is to teach the proper order of the household: "Two or three stinging strokes on the legs or bottom with a switch are usually sufficient to emphasize the point, 'You must obey me.'" But a paragraph later, Dobson insists, "I caution parents not to punish toddlers for behavior which is natural and necessary to learning and development."[9]

Dobson seems to want to have it both ways. He acknowledges that exploration and experimentation are natural for toddlers, but he tells parents not to tolerate what he considers willful defiance. He goes on to describe a hypothetical encounter between parent and child, noting that because a toddler's brain is not developed enough to comprehend a spanking delivered too long after the fact, it must be administered immediately.[10]

This heartbreaking description finds a toddler, moments after being struck by a parent, needing to seek comfort from the person who caused their pain. This is supposed to illustrate proper order being restored in a home. The child's defiance subverts that order, and a swift "administration of justice" is called for. Dobson prescribes good behavior for everyone in the household. Good behavior for the parent is "daring to discipline" a toddler by seemingly harsh but necessary means. For the family to function, *everyone* must be on their best behavior, or the order of the Christian home will break down. Everything, even the child's natural inclination to test limits and assert their will, must be kept in line. Order in the home is a necessary precursor for order in civil society.

Good Behavior as a Social Project

The coupling of the political right's law-and-order agenda with Christian discipline was reinforced by influential evangelist

David Wilkerson, author of *The Cross and the Switchblade* (1963).[11] The book, which recounts Wilkerson's ministry to teen drug addicts and gang members in New York City in the 1950s and early '60s, sold over fifty million copies and was turned into a feature film starring Pat Boone and Erik Estrada in 1970. Wilkerson became a nationally known preacher and evangelist following the success of his book.

Wilkerson's stories were riveting, and they seemed to confirm that America was in accelerating moral decline. Wilkerson, writing in 1963, described the den of iniquity that American Christians feared would spread if left unchecked. He went on to write books on family life like *Parents on Trial* (1967) and *I've Given Up on Parents* (1969) that linked children's disobedience with social delinquency. In his writing and preaching, Wilkerson suggested that parents were ultimately to blame for the teen delinquency he witnessed in his ministry. In Wilkerson's view, it was almost too late for the young people he worked with in the city. They were already criminals and addicts. If only their homes had been places of discipline, of *order*, this pain and suffering could have been avoided.

In *The Christian Family*, Larry Christenson quotes Wilkerson in the chapter "God's Order for Parents" on the problem of a child's "stubbornness" and what it portends. Wilkerson said stubbornness was the one trait observable in "every addict and gang member [he] worked with." He also insisted parents were to blame for leaving children to their stubbornness and recklessness: "Either lazy or unconcerned, our parents today are too soft. Like the priest Eli in the Bible, they allow their children to be neglected by a lack of stern discipline. . . . God will bless parents who restrain their children, and judge those who neglect them."[12]

Christenson heightens proper correction of "disobedience" and "rebellion" to a social good. Fail, and one's children could easily become addicts living on the streets. These extreme stakes are commonly weaponized against Christian parents in books like Christenson's. Over the decades, it became a reliable tactic.

In his book *The Family First* (1972), Kenneth Gangel warned parents that in the current social environment it was more likely than ever that their teens would be tempted to stray: "The behavior of college students nationally was measured with respect to various controversial areas. The results: 50.8% had pre or extramarital sex relations; 36% had taken part in one or more campus demonstrations; 12.5% had broken the law as part of a protest; 31.9% had tried marijuana, and 13.5% had used amphetamines."[13] Gangel, the president of a Christian college, connected the moral decay on college campuses to the polarizing organization Students for a Democratic Society and its political goals.

In 1987, Dobson described the disturbing scenes of youth culture in London to engage a new generation of worried parents: "It is no wonder parents are more concerned in the present era," Dobson wrote in *Parenting Isn't for Cowards*. "Their children are walking through the Valley of the Shadow! Drugs, sex, alcohol, rebellion and deviant lifestyles are everywhere. *What in heaven's name have we allowed to happen to our kids?*"[14]

What have we *allowed* to happen to our kids? Authors like Dobson and Gangel offered anecdotes and observations as evidence that parents had allowed stubbornness and defiance to continue past childhood, growing into full-blown rebellion. The parents, it turns out, had not modeled good behavior. They had been lazy, neglectful, and cowardly.

Christian psychologist Bruce Narramore likewise lamented the spiritual state of young people during the 1960s and '70s, offering insight on why Christian training didn't seem to be "sticking" anymore: "For decades we've thought having a 'Christian home' would insure the stability of our youth. But rampant problems and rebellion among Christian adolescents shoot this theory full of holes. Apparently, there are serious failings, even in our Christian homes. For some reason we have difficulty making our Christian training stick."[15]

Narramore's book *An Ounce of Prevention: A Parent's Guide to Moral and Spiritual Growth of Children*, published by Zondervan in 1973, was an early addition to the growing body of popular Christian parenting literature that followed Dobson's *Dare to Discipline*. The author byline on the cover, "Dr. Bruce Narramore, Psychologist," indicates an awareness of a growing demand for advice and expertise from psychologists—as well as the Christian publishing world's eagerness to provide it.

Like many parenting books of the era, Narramore's opens with a harrowing story, this one involving a teen son who murders his father, described as all the more tragic because they were both reportedly Christians and the father was "active in church."[16] On the next page, he cites an anonymous survey done at a Christian college in which 60 percent of the students indicated that they had smoked marijuana or used another illegal drug within the past year.

"A little of this is normal," writes Narramore, "but we also know of teenagers from well-respected Christian families who have turned completely against the faith and values of their parents. Drug abuse, teenage pregnancies, and heavy drinking are no longer only the distant lifestyles of the non-Christian world. They have planted themselves firmly in the middle of our twentieth-century Christian culture."[17]

Dobson also describes an incident in which a teenage girl attacks her mother and leaves her on the bathroom floor bleeding from a head wound.[18] Bruce Ray, writing in *Withhold Not Correction* (1978), exacerbates parents' fears, asking, "Is it any wonder that in the schools of our land teachers fear for their very lives, lest they be beaten or even *killed* by their students?"[19] These concerns extended parental fears well beyond "What will people think about our family?" to concerns that poorly behaved children were threats to societal—and parental—well-being.

Tim Kimmel, founder of The Hurried Family seminars, wrote his first parenting book, *Legacy of Love: A Plan for Parenting on Purpose*, in 1989 and turned to this well-worn road map of resting the well-being of the nation on the shoulders of parents. He starts by reflecting on a trip to Washington, DC, during which he and millions of others watched the *Challenger* explosion on live television. Unable to focus on his work the day after, he walked to the US Capitol. "Standing on those wide, windswept steps, I was moved to remember that our national future doesn't rest on micro-circuits or the whims of politicians. . . . Someone has stated that the true wealth of a nation is its people. I agree. But I'm inclined to narrow that definition. America's true wealth is its *parents*. . . . Parents are the hinge on which a civilization pivots. They determine whether the door of the future swings open or closed."[20]

Parental behavior is on trial in the public eye and in the invisible gaze of authors like Kimmel. And a child's performance is an indicator of whether parents have been on their best behavior or not.

Failures as Exceptions

Many of these parenting experts give space in their books to the uncomfortable reality that sometimes, without obvious explanation, kids turn away from the faith, have sex, experiment with drugs, or refuse to submit to parental authority. Indeed, it would be cruel not to acknowledge it, even if that acknowledgment rings hollow alongside assurances that proper parenting will bear a particular kind of fruit. Most Christians know families with children who, for no apparent reason, have left the church or "fallen away" in some regard. Is it reasonable to say that there is *always* something parents could have done to prevent a child's struggle or rebellion? That seems like an impossible burden.

Parents tend to look at rebellious children—theirs or someone else's—and ask, "What could have been done to change the outcome?" While virtually every author (in the Christian publishing world and the mainstream) contends that parents are called to teach, discipline, and guide their children, they offer quite varied and often contradictory commentary on what parental failure looks like, and whether there's a clear causal link between parents' behavior and their children's.

There is a small corner of Christian parenting teaching that offers no grace to parents who "fail." Douglas Wilson fully blames parents, reflecting the idea that parents, too, are expected to be held accountable: "Parents of unfaithful children excuse themselves by saying things like, 'We did everything we could.' No sinner ever has the right to say anything like this. . . . The Scriptures teach a direct connection between how children are brought up and how they turn out. When God-fearing parents are confronted with a God-defying child, shame is an entirely appropriate response."[21]

This view also means that "successful" parents can take credit for their children's obedience. In 2023, the Wilsons' parenting advice came under critique, and in response their media arm, Canon Press, sent out an ad defending their parenting resources. They pitched a special bundled discount package on the selling point that "Pastor Wilson's family hasn't had a single apostasy across four generations . . . [or] one black sheep on the outskirts of orthodox biblical Christianity."[22] The ad was retracted the next day.[23]

Most commonly, "failures" of disobedient or faith-rejecting kids are treated as exceptions. And understandably so, given that no one would buy a book dispensing Christian parenting advice if they didn't believe that it would increase their chances of raising well-adjusted Christian kids. Authors of these books have always had to walk a fine line between acknowledging the possibility of failure and arguing that their ideas and methods offer the best chance of success.

Some writers give parents an out, suggesting that the problem is not the parents themselves but the bad advice they have been given. In *Parenting by the Book*, John Rosemond blames child psychologists for misleading mothers: "The psychobabblers . . . have successfully implanted in her head a swarm of 'psychological bogeymen' that cause her to be constantly afraid that one wrong step in her parenting will shatter her child's supposedly fragile psyche. . . . Such is the price we are paying for believing that because people have capital letters after their names, they know what they are talking about."[24]

Margie Lewis, author of *The Hurting Parent* (1980), offers a more circumspect and therapeutic perspective. She writes that parents who felt they were failing could find little comfort in many Christian parenting books:

> I could walk into any Christian bookstore and buy half a truckload of books on the Christian family. . . . It seems every Christian psychologist and half of the ministers in North America have recorded their advice on how we can successfully raise our children in the nurture of the Lord and see them joyously line up behind us to march in the great army of Christ. But what can we do if we didn't read these books until it was too late? What can we do if we followed all those principles and guidelines for Christian parenthood and they just didn't seem to work?[25]

Lewis, a longtime executive secretary at Asbury Theological Seminary, wrote the book with contributions from her son, Gregg, the editor of *Campus Life* magazine. Lewis's book received a cover blurb from Ruth Graham, who indicated that many Christian parents are afraid to discuss their failures openly because of "the strong disapproval of some Christians who have never entered into that part of God's suffering."

Lewis mostly shares stories of families, rarely with a word of condemnation toward parents or children. She offers case studies and examples alongside Scripture, with some devotional words on the importance of forgiveness and unconditional love. She also quotes Longfellow, Horace Bushnell, Seneca, and Shakespeare.

Reading *The Hurting Parent* is a bit like reading Ecclesiastes or Job; it's an honest account of human pain and suffering with no attempt to answer the question "Why?" Lewis muses here and there that many parents wish they had done certain things differently, but ultimately she focuses on the parents' spiritual health. Rather than *prescribing* parental behavior with the intent of shaping child behavior, Lewis *encourages* parents to look inward and deal with their own questions and pain, not as a means to a child-behavior-related end but as a way to heal.

Taking a different approach, megachurch pastor Chuck Swindoll admonishes parents to stand firm in the face of rebellion. When there is an impasse, Swindoll writes in *The Strong Family* (1991), a behavior or rebellion that simply cannot be quashed, a parent is to remain, above all, *in charge*:

> Let me give it to you straight: Parents, it is our mandate to deal firmly with rebellion. It will be unpleasant and difficult. It will always be heartrending, and on occasion you will think that you may lose your mind. But *you must stand firm*. . . . At such times, you either remain the authority or you relinquish that position and open the door to a miserable existence in which your entire family lives under siege. You may come to the place where you will wonder if you should call for professional help . . . or assistance from civil or police authorities. If it comes to that, you must act in the best interest of your family. You are

> the parent. You cannot afford to allow your authority in the home to be undermined.[26]

Swindoll goes on to describe the "tragic, pathetic sight" of parents who allow their rebellious children to wreak havoc on the family with the wry observation, "That situation didn't happen overnight. It was years in the making."[27]

Swindoll offers cold comfort to families facing seemingly uncontrollable rebellion. He refuses to give parents an out, insisting that *something*, at some point, allowed a child to start spiraling out of control—even if that something was subtle or accidental or simply a failure to maintain authority. In the end, parents reap what they sow and must at the very least hold their heads high and maintain authority. Parental behavior, he insists, should remain in line with the chain of command.

At the end of the chapter titled "Confronting the Unpleasant," Swindoll stops just short of suggesting that parents bear full responsibility for the rebellion of their children. However, he also doesn't acknowledge that children, as autonomous humans, may simply choose to diverge from the path desired by parents. The closing takeaway Swindoll offers is telling: "*If the level of rebellion necessitates a separation, you must choose principle over person.*"[28] With that guidance, he elaborates on the importance of preserving the family unit and the order of the home. "I don't care how old or how gifted the child may be, no rebel is worth the destruction of a family unit. No matter the background, no matter how intimidating, no matter how violent, no matter how manipulative, or how much trouble it may be to confront the unpleasant, a rebel must not be allowed to ruin a home. . . . If there is a principle at stake, no matter what the relationship, you stand on the principle."[29]

Swindoll uses the example of the prodigal son to reinforce the idea that sometimes separation is necessary. Though nothing in Jesus's story suggests that the father has allowed his son to persist in a rebellious streak or that the father has initiated the separation, Swindoll tells parents to consider cutting off their children. If a child is too far gone, if parents can't rein in the rebellion, they must salvage their authority in the home and preserve the order of the household. And parents seem to have followed this advice. We heard from many survey respondents who described painful parent-initiated estrangement when adult children failed to live up to standards of obedience. Sometimes this included being cut off from younger siblings to forestall bad influences.

We often talk about the shame many children experienced in homes steeped in Christian parenting literature, but we talk less about the shame heaped on parents. Christian parents reading these books were pummeled with frightening accounts of children caught up in drugs or violence or teen pregnancy. Authors implored them to establish authority, compel obedience, and help fight the battle against secular humanism and social decay through their families.

Good behavior—child behavior and parental behavior—would establish families as outposts of God's kingdom. And in a secularizing, chaotic world, God's kingdom needs strongholds where the family unit is intact and its members are in line. The family that failed was essentially dead weight. The needs of the family always superseded the needs of the individual. Such a framework left little room for consideration of children's unique needs and desires, or even their humanity.

5

ARE CHILDREN HUMAN?

The Rights, Autonomy, and Vulnerability of Children

Henry Cloud and John Townsend's book *Boundaries: When to Say Yes, How to Say No to Take Control of Your Life* has sold over four million print copies. It was first published in 1992 and is number twenty-five on *Christianity Today*'s 2006 list of books that have shaped evangelicals.[1] *Boundaries* has helped Cloud and Townsend build a resource empire, including a spin-off book, *Boundaries with Kids: When to Say Yes, When to Say No, to Help Your Children Gain Control of Their Lives* (1998).

In the introduction, Cloud and Townsend write, "[This] book is organized around key concepts that will help children take control of their lives."[2] Unlike many other Christian parenting books, it focuses on a child's individual will and autonomy. *Boundaries with Kids* didn't reach the bestseller list, but it applies many of the same principles and big ideas from *Boundaries* to help parents maintain limits with children and teach their children to hold boundaries in their own relationships.

Anyone reading mainstream parenting literature from the 2020s will immediately recognize the language of boundaries. Becky Kennedy, a family therapist and author of the bestselling book *Good Inside* (2022), speaks often about setting clear and "sturdy" expectations about what a parent will do in a particular situation and focusing on what parents can control rather than on controlling child behavior. For parents operating outside a Christian worldview, the language of boundaries has proven useful in addressing unwanted behaviors without the use of moral categories.

Cloud and Townsend also encourage parents to focus on what they can control and to make peace with the fact that their children, as dependent as they may be on their parents, are individuals who can't be controlled: "This book is geared much more toward how you, the parent, behave with your child than toward educating your child. Learning boundaries has a lot to do with going through experiences, such as receiving consequences for behavior, learning to take ownership, and dealing with the boundaries of others."[3]

Their articulation of boundaries seems to conflict with James Dobson's insistence in *Dare to Discipline* that parents can and must require their children's respect: "Developing respect for the parents is the critical factor in child management," and "Respect for parents must be maintained."[4]

While most parents would agree that they desire the respect of their children, whether it is something that can be forced, required, maintained, or controlled is a different question.

Tedd Tripp's book *Shepherding a Child's Heart* (1995) is full of admonitions to parents to probe their children's hearts and uncover sin, a perspective that bumps up against Cloud and Townsend's ideas about boundaries. Tripp's approach is one of spiritual enmeshment, in which parents are tasked with taking on the role of the Holy Spirit—uncovering sinful desires and labeling a child's motives—rather than allowing the child's inner life to remain their own, private and known by God alone. "When you direct, correct, or discipline, you are not acting out of your own will, you are acting on behalf of God," Tripp writes. "You don't have to wonder if it is okay for you to be in charge. You certainly do not need your child's permission. God has given you a duty to perform, therefore the endorsement of your child is not necessary."[5]

By contrast, Cloud and Townsend write about parents enforcing boundaries and helping kids come to understand their own boundaries and confidently hold them. For some Christian parents, the idea of encouraging children to assert themselves conflicts with long-standing teaching about the "breaking" or "bending" of a child's will. Allowing a child to ask a parent not to touch their hair or read their diary seems like granting that child authority over the parent. And in some cases, the boundaries a child would like to enforce aren't age appropriate (such as a child who wants unlimited access to the internet without parental controls).

Bringing ethical frameworks into Christian parenting complicates the long-standing assumption that parental authority is *the* overarching principle. A system that relies on parental authority above all else is clear and simple. It requires a parent to resist being overly moved by a child's desires, preferences, or needs. "So-called modern methods of child-raising make much of a child's intuitive sense of right and wrong, of fairness and unfairness," writes Larry Christenson in *The Christian Family*. "Great burden is laid upon the parent to deal fairly with the child. . . . Something as important as a child's obedience cannot be made to hinge upon the perfection of a parent's judgment in every situation. . . . The child's responsibility is simply to obey."[6] The burden of dealing fairly with a child is, in Christenson's view, too much for a parent to bear in every circumstance. Obedience, not fairness, is the right goal. And if fairness happens to be convenient enough for the parent, so be it.

Christian philosopher Nicholas Wolterstorff notes that empathy is perhaps one of the most powerful animators of justice and fairness and that dehumanizing the vulnerable and oppressed causes people to shut down their empathetic responses.[7] Some might balk at the suggestion that children in loving Christian homes are "oppressed," but it's hard to argue that they are not incredibly *vulnerable*. In our world, children rely on their parents and other adults for survival, and they have little power to change their circumstances or advocate for themselves in a world that centers adults. That reality should move us toward empathy and concern for their fair treatment. But Christenson cautions parents not to be controlled by their desire to empathize with their child's "intuitive sense of right and wrong." It's just too risky and too unstructured. Such negotiations might make it difficult to maintain a home in which there is no question about who is in charge at all times.

To deal ethically with children is to be willing to be moved by their desires, needs, and preferences. It doesn't mean letting children always have their way, but it does require parents to value a child's perspective rather than reduce their agency to the binary choice between obedience and disobedience. Theologian Bonnie Miller-McLemore writes, "Children must be fully respected as persons, valued as gifts, and viewed as agents."[8] The ethical treatment of children means leaving behind a framework of rules based solely on hierarchy.

Cloud and Townsend offer practical ways to apply a "law of respect" in the home that affords children agency and separateness. They encourage parents to hold boundaries with a dose of both "reality and empathy,"[9] and they emphasize that parental modeling is more important than the administration of consequences for disobedience. "A child's need to belong is more central than his need to be good," claim Cloud and Townsend, pushing back on the idea that obedience is a child's highest calling and acknowledging that children will act in ways that get the attention of their caregivers.[10] Children, like adults, are made for community and belonging, Cloud and Townsend argue. Empathizing with their desire for belonging rather than insisting on compliance humanizes children and reorients parental perception.

For some, the very suggestion that parents ought to look to an extrabiblical ethical framework to guide their parenting seems to impose an authority higher than Scripture, and for many evangelicals, that is a nonstarter, especially in a time when partisan politics have pushed human rights and social justice into broad categories closely associated with the left wing. Rights language is often used by progressives to advocate for social norms in a direction many evangelicals think is morally wrong.[11] Empathy itself is under scrutiny from a small group of conservative Christians like Joe Rigney (author of *Leadership and Emotional Sabotage*) and Allie Beth Stuckey (author of *Toxic Empathy*), who insist that empathy has been corrupted by the left and, as such, cannot move us toward love and right relationship.[12]

In the internet age, even parents who are wary of rights and social justice frameworks might nonetheless consider ethics when it comes to children. As it becomes apparent that children's attention is a product and their data can easily be compromised, any parent with a social media account must decide whether it is responsible to post and share pictures publicly without their children's permission. Furthermore, can children even consent to stories being shared about them or their image being posted to the internet? Christian parenting writers and teachers rely on anecdotes to frame their advice in print, some from their own families. Influencers and family vloggers put their children's images, voices, and stories online to build their platforms (this is, of course, not unique to the Christian influencer sphere). Footage and photos of children eating, crying, or playing accompany posts from influencers, illustrating everything from inspiration for family holiday celebrations to discipline methods. In the United States, there are few legal structures in place to protect children from exploitation online at the hands of their parents.

Books like Cloud and Townsend's *Boundaries with Kids*, while not perfect, provide a contrast to Christian parenting books that insist a child's will and affections can and should be *controlled*. Lurking beneath a phrase like "your children *must* respect you" is the implication that respect can be forced. In the same way, the expectation for obedience "all the way, right away, and with a happy heart" is actually a claim that a parent can and should require a child to *be happy*. It's a claim that a child's inner life is not actually their own. It's a claim that calls into question a child's autonomy and personhood, and even their humanity.

A Vocabulary of Dignity

Apologist Ken Ham recounts the following anecdote in his 2006 parenting book, *Raising Godly Children in an Ungodly World*: "I remember visiting the hospital in Australia where my sister had just had a baby. I looked at this beautiful infant and said, 'What a beautiful looking sinful creature you have there!' (I was thinking of Jeremiah 17:9 that says, 'The heart is deceitful above all things and desperately wicked, who can know it?') I was nearly thrown out of the hospital, as you might imagine, but when they took this baby home, it didn't take the parents long to find out I was right!"[13]

This exchange is offered as a lighthearted example of what it looks like to retain a wise and vigilant posture toward children. They might be cute, beautiful even, but they are, at their core, sinful creatures. His remark in the recovery room to a mother and her newborn might have been socially awkward, but, in his view, he was at least theologically correct. Ham claims that after a few days at home with this "creature," the parents agreed with him.

Ham is best known as the founder of Answers in Genesis, an organization that advocates for young-earth creationism. He devotes much of his book on parenting to the subject of education—homeschooling in particular. He refers to children as "vessels" that can easily become contaminated by secular ideas. "Our children are not 'good,'" Ham writes. "They have sinful natures and fleshly tendencies that make them highly vulnerable to temptation and compromise."[14]

Ham also speaks about the importance of *training* children instead of merely *teaching* them. The distinction he seems to be making between training and teaching has to do with posture: both the posture of the parents doing the instruction and the posture they are expecting their children to have as Christians. Ham argues that Christianity is to be presented as the only logical and obvious explanation for the world and that all instruction is to flow from this assertion, with anything else treated as error. "Parents are to train children in the truth of Scripture, giving no options. For a Christian, it is not that truth is the *best* policy. . . . Truth is the *only* policy. Children who are merely *taught* can hear other teaching and easily depart from truth because of their sinful flesh and their bias against God. . . . We must diligently *train* them in truth, condemning error for what it is."[15]

Why use the word "train"? Why is "teach" inadequate? Ham tells parents to offer no options, no other possible explanations for the natural world or the workings of human society than what the Bible gives us. We can assume Ham uses the word "training" as a way to reference Proverbs 22:6 and for its association with behaviorism. Behaviorism explores how people learn through conditioning, which involves offering a system of rewards and consequences that powerfully incentivizes certain choices for the person being trained, to the point that decision-making becomes involuntary. We train our pets according to the principles of behaviorism; we reward tricks like "sit" and "roll over" with a treat, and we punish unwanted behaviors, such as barking, with squirt bottles or rolled up newspapers. When parents train children this way, they seek a practical outcome: Good behaviors will become automatic, and bad ones will eventually disappear.

When it comes to education, emphasizing training and downplaying the effectiveness of teaching reveal a very anti-humanist view of learning. In Ham's estimation, Christian education should condition a child so that any new information they encounter first runs through the filter imposed by their training. Before a child is allowed to engage with the world, they must first be trained to see the world in a particular way. And the stakes, as usual, are high: "God is a gracious God and forgives, but the consequences of your actions will still be part of the legacy you leave . . . and you only have one opportunity to leave it, so you better be doing it as you should. If God's people do not produce godly offspring, then the application of the truth of God's Word will be severely and negatively impacted for generations to come."[16]

For Ham, training children is a social project with cosmic consequences. Ham's articulation of what it means to train children ventures quite close to the definition of indoctrination. Indoctrination is never just one thing, one piece of media, one strategy: Indoctrination is a goal. The ultimate end of indoctrination is to impose a belief system or worldview on someone, usually by restricting access to information, so only that which reinforces the desired belief system is available. Indoctrination is unethical because it strips children of autonomy. It is distinct from teaching, or even persuasion, because it involves strategically removing access to information that would allow a learner to ask questions, evaluate sources, or consider alternatives.

Raising a child in a faith community is not necessarily indoctrination. Every human being has a worldview that begins to take shape during childhood. It is dishonest to suggest that it is possible to raise a child without helping them form their worldview. Ham's vision of education approaches indoctrination because it severely restricts a child's social and intellectual world. He advocates for homeschooling because "it is impossible to train children under a worldly system and then add God to it" and because "it is too easy to lose saltiness in an unsalty environment."[17]

Among the dehumanizing things Ham says about children throughout his book, perhaps the one that best sums up his view of them is this: "Children are not miniature adults. They are unable to discriminate between good and evil. They don't have the discipline to choose between truth and the cleverly crafted evolutionary philosophies."[18]

This impoverished view of children's ability to assess the world around them speaks to a deep ambivalence about their feelings, experiences, and desires. Here, Ham's point centers on their inability to discern between truth and misinformation. But in service of making his point, he paints children in a particularly unflattering light, encouraging parents to see children as utterly senseless when it comes to discerning good and evil in the world around them.

What does it mean to say that children can't recognize good in the world? Do we really believe that God doesn't imbue children with the ability to see beauty, experience joy, feel deep love and affection, and *know* beyond a doubt that those things are good?

When children experience the loving care of their mother, are they unable to sense and know that their mother's love is *good*? Are we to think that what they are experiencing is just a biological reaction? An animal instinct? Is there no divine spark in them that recognizes the grace of familial love as a gift from God?

All humans must continually discern between wisdom and foolishness, between good and evil. It is true that we are all fallible and prone to lapses in judgment. We all fail to recognize the goodness and beauty and wisdom in God's creation, and we are all capable of ignoring or becoming numb to evil. Ham's appraisal of children's capacity for discernment may be polemical hyperbole, but even so, he seems to be suggesting that children are something less than human, only capable of understanding cause and effect.

Ham isn't the only writer to use phrases or metaphors to describe children in a way that minimizes their individuality and capacity for reason and spiritual experience. Preacher Voddie Baucham famously claimed, in reference to young children, "That's a viper in a diaper," which drew big laughs from his congregation and was repeated in later publications.[19] In *The Strong-Willed Child*, James Dobson says that "a well-deserved spanking often turn[s] a sullen little troublemaker into a sweet and loving angel."[20] On both ends of Dobson's behaviorist spectrum, there is a dehumanizing descriptor: "troublemaker" and "angel."

It may seem odd to suggest that calling a child an angel is dehumanizing, but consider the implications of that label. It puts the child in a category of total compliance, total goodness. No human is angelic, and angels aren't human to begin with. The best version of a child isn't for them to be as close to an angel as possible; it's for them to be a fully human child, beloved by Jesus and bearing the image of God.

We realize that sermons and popular nonfiction and self-help books will often include hyperbole and humor to make a point. These are effective rhetorical devices, engaging parents who are exasperated with a particular phase in their child's development or leaving readers with a memorable takeaway. But decades of Christian parenting books that take this approach—that use humor or extreme overstatement to garner a chuckle from parents at the expense of their kids—have left many Christian families with a twisted view of relationships and a diminished view of children.

Beings of Value

Catholic writer Dorothy Sayers wrote, "What is repugnant to every human being is to be reckoned always as a member of a class and not as an individual person."[21] Many parenting books reckon with children as a class, in that they are written *about* children *for* parents. In the interest of offering generalized advice, each child disappears into a nameless and faceless grouping—a member of the class "children." The generalizations in parenting books are necessary for the existence of such a genre, but on close examination it becomes clear that many of the general claims about the nature of children, and even some of the categories created to describe them (strong-willed, for example), are dehumanizing and flattening.

To label a child "strong-willed" and prescribe responses to their behavior according to that label is to dismiss the possibility that there is something valid and distinct about their particular response to the world. Maybe a "strong-willed" child isn't responding with anger because they are just stubborn by nature; maybe their sense of being unjustly treated has merit. Parenting guidance can help make sense of an individual child's behavior, imparting a sense of relief for those who feel like they are the only one facing a particular challenge. However, a parent can very easily let the scripts and explanations offered by a professed expert dictate their responses to the child in front of them. Labels like "strong-willed" can inadvertently influence parents to dismiss behavior as part of their child's programming rather than as a form of communication. Parenting books are not user manuals, and children aren't computers to be troubleshot and programmed.

Some authors are more circumspect as they generalize about children, at least providing caveats about considering every child's unique needs. But several of them discourage parents from seeing their children as exceptions to the rules. The individuality of a child never supersedes a biblical model or principle, or to restate Chuck Swindoll's words, "You must choose the principle over the person."[22]

Despite authors' use of terms like "tyrants" and "dictators" to describe children (particularly toddlers), it's worth restating that children are a highly vulnerable group in our world. Public spaces are not built for them, they don't have their own political representation, and while child labor laws have proliferated in some places, child exploitation remains a global concern. Children rely on adult guardians for housing, food, and clothing. They rely on adults to see to their health and safety and to monitor their physical growth and well-being.

In the ancient world, women and children were not perceived as human in the way that able-bodied men were considered human. Christians living under the authority of the Roman Empire knew and experienced this to a degree that we can barely imagine. "The unproductive are those who are unfit for any kind of work, private or public, because of old age, bodily infirmity, insanity, or some other excusing cause," wrote Syrianos, a military engineer of the Byzantine Empire in his treatise on war strategy. Historian Nadya Williams notes that while women and children aren't explicitly named in Syrianos's list of the "unproductive" members of society, they are undoubtedly implied—particularly by the terms "bodily infirmity" and "insanity."[23]

Children were needed for the future health of the empire, even though they were a drain on resources (and high mortality rates made outcomes uncertain).[24] Contrast this posture with Jesus's demeanor. He welcomed children and celebrated their dependent, unproductive, oppressed position in society, and in so doing he dignified them as they were, not as they would someday be. "Then children were being brought to him in order that he might lay his hands on them and pray. The disciples spoke sternly to those who brought them, but Jesus said, 'Let the children come to me, and do not stop them, for it is to such as these that the kingdom of heaven belongs.' And he laid his hands on them and went on his way" (Matt. 19:13–15 NRSVue).

The disciples chastise the caregivers in this vignette, not the children themselves. But Jesus says to let them come, turning his attention to the children and their agency, their movement toward him, toward his hands, toward his blessing.

"Do not stop them," Jesus says. There is a change in focus. As the disciples reprove parents for bringing children—perhaps they were quiet and reverent or perhaps they were noisy and excited, the text doesn't say—Jesus turns his attention to the children coming into his view and welcomes them. Children have access to the person of Christ: intimate, immediate, unfettered access.

Christ and Child, Christ as Child

Episodes that include encounters between Jesus and children in the Gospels—Jesus welcoming children in Matthew 9 and the healing of Jairus's daughter in Mark 5, for example—show that Jesus was willing to engage with the least powerful. Some theologians go a step further, suggesting that in developing a uniquely Christian understanding of children we should look not only to situations where Jesus was *with* children but also at the fact that Jesus *was* a child.

R. L. Stollar recommends meditating on Christ as a child to deepen our understanding of God's sense of justice: "When

Christians read stories from the Tanakh that describe God's righteous anger toward human abuse and oppression, we often think that God is showing the anger of a parent toward their children. . . . When adults believe that God's anger toward human abuse and oppression justifies their own anger toward their children's misbehavior, it can lead to child abuse."[25]

For Christians whose theology emphasizes God's power, sovereignty, and transcendence, flipping the script can be uncomfortable. God as Father is, for many of us, the most familiar relational reference. I (Kelsey) remember the first time I sang the song "I Am a Friend of God" in church. After the service, I talked with my mother about how it felt strange to call God a friend and to sing the line "He calls me friend." She pointed me to John 15:15, where Jesus tells his disciples, "I have called you friends." Still, something about the song, even into adulthood, felt overly familiar, not reverent enough. I am a friend of God? He calls me friend? How do I square that with my understanding of God the father, God the creator, a God of justice?

For some adult children, the transition to friendship with their parents can be fraught, even seemingly impossible. Relationships built on power aren't easily reoriented, especially when they rest on a hierarchy said to reflect God's created order for human beings. A willingness to conform to and thrive in these hierarchical relationships proves a person's ability to live in relationship with God. This is one reason why some conservative Christians bristle at references to God as mother, since in the Christian family hierarchy the mother is subordinate.

Stollar does not suggest that God as child replaces or supersedes God as father; rather, he suggests that meditating on the childness of God as young Jesus can help parents differentiate between God's righteous anger and the anger they feel when their children exasperate them.

One often unspoken reason why it can be so hard for parents to give up spanking is that anything less feels inadequate in the face of the rage they may feel toward their children in the heat of the moment.[26] That rage can feel visceral, convincing a parent that there *must* be a righteous reason for their anger, that their anger reflects God's cosmic desire for justice and order. Swift and painful retribution in the form of a spanking *feels* just and merited for the parent who is at their wit's end or believes that it would be unjust *not* to punish.[27] For a parent who feels their role and authority parallels that of almighty God, an affront to that authority is a punishable offense.

Parental anger, suggests Stollar, finds a satisfying place to land when a parent believes their anger reflects God's anger. But this mental framework shrinks God's anger down to a neatly packaged human experience. He writes:

> God's anger cannot be reduced to or compared to parental anger. God's anger also includes the anger of children. God is Child, too! And as a Triune God who rages against human abuse and oppression, God rages most against those who have the power to abuse and oppress. This would imply that God identifies more with the powerless children than with the powerful adults, which is in line with what the Jewish prophets and Christian liberation theologians teach us. We find God on the underside of history, where the powerless and the oppressed are. So too we find God with the children. . . . God is not an angry patriarch.[28]

This theological reframe invites Christians to see the meeting of heaven and earth in God's entrance into our suffering and into the suffering of the oppressed—including the suffering of children. The most loving parents sometimes struggle to contend with their children as humans of equal dignity and value. They have individual wills, but their capacity for reasoning and decision-making isn't fully developed. They react to stimuli differently than adults do.

Think about the children in your life. Say a four-year-old wakes up in the morning and comes down for breakfast. She asks, “Can I have some oatmeal?” That basic request could be met with, “Sorry, honey, I’m busy” or “We don’t have any oatmeal today” or “Go ask your mom.” To be a child is to have a will, personality, and imagination but almost no agency in the world beyond what their parents are willing to give them. Children are fully human but profoundly limited in their ability to self-actualize.

The limitations of children in some ways reflect the limitations God imposed on himself to enter the suffering of humanity. It was not beneath God to embrace the dependence of an infant, then a child, then a teenager. It was not beneath God in the person of Jesus to take on realities of infancy and childhood on earth. This mind-bending reality not only humanizes Christ but also dignifies children.

Children’s Rights or Parental Rights?

Evangelical parenting advice emphasizes God-given authority and hierarchy. As a result, it naturally follows that many writers and teachers suggest that permissive parenting leads to a world where children have the run of things and we are all at their mercy.[29]

Gary and Anne Marie Ezzos’ *Baby Wise* method warns that parents shouldn’t let their children become the family dictators. A baby’s needs—sleeping, eating, attention—should be subsumed by the parents’ schedule and routine. This was viewed as necessary in order to begin the process of instilling self-control and respect for authority from birth. Many Christian parenting books exhibit concern about the power children appear to exert over their parents’ emotions and the order of a household. Heather Creekmore, writing about her regret for using Gary Ezzo’s and Robert Bucknam’s methods, reveals the influence this messaging initially had on her: "[*Baby Wise*] convinced me (temporarily) that the problems in the world today are created by how 'baby-centric' parents become. Since I didn't want to raise a selfish child, it only made sense to demand this creation of mine to fall in line."[30]

In *Dare to Discipline*, Dobson tells story after story of parent-child conflict in which a parent struggles to get the upper hand, to "win," and the language of parents "winning" is a staple in countless other resources. If a child "wins" a perceived power struggle, this is extrapolated as an indicator of future rebellion and selfishness.

But this fear of raising selfish, controlling children is undercut by the reality that children are at the mercy of their caretakers. Even in loving homes, they have very limited power. Children have never had the upper hand over their parents, no matter how harried the parents may feel. One myth of Christian parenting resources is that parents can somehow avoid the hard reality that they cannot control their children. No matter how strongly parents feel the pressure to raise "good kids" who reflect well on their family, a child's behavior and feelings belong to the child. Parents undoubtedly have influence over their children, but that influence is inexact and unpredictable.

Historian Steven Mintz notes that social panics over child behavior put youth under a microscope while ignoring the important broader context of the world in which they are growing up: "Our society tends to treat young people's problems separately from those of adults, as if they were not interconnected phenomena. We hold youth to perfectionistic standards that adults are not expected to meet. In fact, young people's behavior tends to parallel that of adults."[31]

Children and their parents don't inhabit two separate worlds. Their struggles are ours. We all contend with feelings of guilt and shame. Remembering that can help parents raise children with a sense of moral responsibility and agency in the world—without saddling them with the same kind of shame and self-doubt.

In 1972, Christian psychologist Bruce Narramore wrote, "If we are to accomplish our desires as Christian parents, we must zero in on our own behavior and our own methods of Christian training. Christian training will work if it's really *biblical* training."[32] A little over a decade later, reflecting back, Narramore revisited the subject in his book *No Condemnation: Rethinking Guilt Motivation in Preaching, Counseling, and Parenting* (1984): "I became convinced that the guilt feelings experienced by some Christians are actually compounded by a misunderstanding of the biblical role of guilt and conscience in the Christian life. Instead of realizing that the processes we know as guilt and conscience were distorted by the Fall, we tend to accept them as divine conviction. Consequently, we heap unneeded condemnation on ourselves and other sensitive people and impose a burden that interferes with the freedom we could have in Christ."[33]

Narramore concludes that all the emphasis on behavior and sin nature is, in some ways, treating guilt as the first principle, the ultimate reality of being human. He invites the reader to consider whether our preoccupation with sin—our sin and the sin of others—is actually a symptom of fallenness. The freedom we have in Christ, not our sin and guilt, ought to be the first principle, the central element of human identity. And our children deserve to know it too.

6

SINNERS FROM THEIR MOTHERS' WOMBS

Children, Sin, and Atonement

> Sin was a constant part of my reality. I was always dealing with the process of rooting it out or getting it rooted out of my heart. I remember as a kid one time, thinking about the world of Winnie the Pooh, and thinking, *They are so fortunate* (*we were not allowed to say lucky!*) . . . *they can just live their lives and not worry about sin all the time because I guess they don't have God or the Bible in their world.*
>
> —anonymous survey respondent

Pause for a moment and ask yourself, "What is 'sin'?" How would you describe it to someone else? How did you first learn to define it? People who grew up in American evangelical communities may respond with something like this: Sin is missing the mark of God's righteousness or "All have sinned and fallen short of the glory of God" (Rom. 3:23).

Let's consider how these popular definitions of sin apply to parenting. What "mark" do children miss? How do children in particular fall short of the glory of God? What does it mean when someone says that children are "sinners," and what are parents expected to do about it? We heard from many people whose family lives were permeated with unspoken assumptions about "sin nature," the idea that humans are born into and inclined toward sin.

> A lot of thought and talk about sin nature and how to overcome it was always present, especially with babies and toddlers. As a family, we always laughed about the toddler's little sin nature and understood that our parents saw their God-given jobs as conquering it.
>
> —Carmen

Christian teaching identifies the fall, when Adam and Eve disobeyed God, as the moment sin inescapably entered the world. The theological concept of original sin describes how every human being since is now tainted by the impurity, death, and power of sin. Theologians over the centuries grappled with how this applied to children: Are children born fully human? When does a child become a human being? And what does it mean to be human? Is it soul, spirit, and body? And which elements are impacted by sin? A theologian's conclusions were shaped by their unique time in history and prevailing beliefs about life, death, and conception.

Tertullian, for example, wrote during the second century about how God mysteriously worked with human sperm to make it into a human being. He offers no perception of the role of women in reproduction. Others believed that God imparted the human soul directly to the body at some point (theologians disagreed on exactly when) or that life began at quickening or first breath. They saw this as an echo of God breathing life into Adam, which is quite different from the view that many evangelicals hold today—that a human soul arrives at conception.[1]

While Christians have almost universally agreed that the human condition is in some way fallen and in need of salvation and repair, different corners of the church have different emphases. Generally speaking, the Eastern church is comparatively hopeful about the human condition and free will. The Western church, with its Roman Catholic legacy and subsequent Reformed denominations, is heavily influenced by Augustine and his prolific writings about human depravity.

Theologians might agree that everyone is born under a curse and in need of purification, but that is different from imputing individual moral guilt, or "culpability," to people. Cyprian believed that "even a newborn child who has never committed actual sin . . . by his first nativity has contracted the contagion of the ancient death."[2] However, Clement "vehemently denies that a newborn baby which has not performed any act of its own can have fallen under the curse of Adam."[3] Some church fathers saw the unfallen Edenic Adam and Eve as being in a kind of childlike state. In the seventh century, Isidore of Seville came up with a classification of childhood that was used and employed up until the Reformation: Infancy was birth to age seven (and innocent); boyhood was age seven to fourteen (and children were seen as capable of good and evil); age fourteen to twenty-eight was a kind of adolescent precursor to adulthood, and youths of this age could be prosecuted under Canon Law.[4]

Our intention here is not to attempt to identify the "right" theological perspective but instead to point out the diversity of perspectives within the Christian tradition and highlight the fact that these ideas developed over time. Theology, particularly regarding ideas that neither Scripture nor church tradition speaks clearly on, is an imprecise endeavor. That fact alone should sober the pastor-teachers who so easily describe children and toddlers as "sinners."

The Sin of Being a Child

I remember my youth pastor, after the birth of his fourth child, joked that she was "just a little sin bag, but a very cute sin bag."

—Elise

Most evangelical resources assume their target audience knows what sin is and accepts that children—whatever their age—are sinners. As a result, "sin" frequently becomes an umbrella term for everything parents don't like, from tantrums to sibling conflict to misbehavior. If resources do include a discussion of sin, it's often presuppositional. For example, Ginger Hubbard tells parents that to understand sin nature, parents must accept that their child is born sinful, that sin is bound up in their hearts, and that sin is not a laughing matter.[5]

Hubbard's discussion of these three points uses the words "folly" and "disobedience" as synonyms for sin, and the key circular takeaway is that children are sinful, and this is why they disobey. "This [original sin]," Hubbard writes, "explains why a room full of toddlers do not have to be taught how to fight over a toy. They just know."[6]

We also came across resources that discuss sin in the abstract alongside teaching that interprets childlikeness as an outgrowth of sin. J. Richard Fugate, who describes himself as a self-taught theologian, writes, "When sin entered the world, mankind . . . became separated from God, subject to death, and under judicial sentence of the all-righteous God."[7] Fugate goes on to state that the fallout from human disobedience is death, spiritual deadness, and eternal damnation. Fugate then leaps to apply this abstract concept of sin to childlikeness and immaturity: "Every sweet, innocent, cuddly baby possesses within his flesh the constant temptation to fulfill the strong desire of sin. . . . He wants what he wants when he wants it. A child wants to be fed what and when he wishes, to have the total attention of others, to play always, and generally to have his every desire fulfilled without regard for anyone else."[8]

For Fugate, a child's innate self-centeredness—"he wants what he wants when he wants it"—reflects his sin nature. But on what grounds? Why is a childlike state of dependency, which according to Christian understanding is part of God's design in growing from immaturity to maturity, "sinful"? Is a newborn baby longing for milk in the night *sinful*? Surely Jesus, the only person to have lived a human life without sin, cried for milk as an infant. Is it *sinful* for a dependent child to seek to have their needs and wants filled? Bruce Ray, author of *Withhold Not Correction*, writes about the lying cries of a newborn baby "pretending" to be hurt. "When mother inspects," Ray says, "there is nothing binding him, nothing pricking him, his diapers are clean, there is nothing to irritate him, and that cry which sounded like a cry of hurt was actually nothing more than a cry of anger." Ray connects this to original sin, and he goes on to say that this baby "as soon as it is capable of any sort of expression, speaks lies. Then, too, when he begins to speak words, he begins to speak lies."[9]

Viewpoints like Fugate's and Ray's dishonor God's creative design and diminish the glory of the incarnation: They (1) equate sin nature with personal moral failure and culpability, (2) ascribe adult motives to infants, who have no sense of self or parental other, and (3) interpret anything short of perfection as sin. These ideas are out of sync with what the church has historically practiced regarding infant baptism, where children born into Christian households were presented as washed and clean of original sin. The state of original sin was not something found in an infant's cry or any specific action they took but in their humanity, and original sin was dealt with through baptism.[10]

Infant baptism raises practical questions: What happens to infants who aren't baptized? At what age are they culpable for their misdeeds? If children who haven't willfully sinned die, are they forever separated from God or sent to hell? You won't find theologians agreeing about *when* a child becomes aware of their guilt and wrongdoing, but, generally speaking, they do accept the idea of an age of accountability, a moment of moral development when a child understands right from wrong. Until that point, children are in a state of innocence from culpability or willful wrongdoing. Only after this point are they considered responsible for their behavior.[11]

Parenting authors who write about six- and seven-year-old "white-washed tombs" (in reference to Matt. 23:27) or a baby whose "cries are lies" are far down the theological path of "total depravity." Jonathan Edwards's famous sermon "Sinners in the Hands of an Angry God" sparked the First Great Awakening (a time of religious fervor followed by mass conversion/revival) in American Christianity. It represents a pivotal point in American spiritual formation and has influenced many evangelical families through the efforts of John Piper—an Edwards devotee—and Desiring God ministries.

In the sermon, Edwards describes how offensive sin and sinful humanity is to a holy God:

> The God that holds you over the pit of hell, much as one holds a spider, or some loathsome insect over the fire, abhors you, and is dreadfully provoked: his wrath towards you burns like fire; he looks upon you as worthy of nothing else, but to be cast into the fire; he is of purer eyes than to bear to have you in his sight; you are ten thousand times more abominable in his eyes than the most hateful venomous serpent is in ours. You have offended him infinitely more than ever a stubborn rebel did his prince; and yet it is nothing but his hand that holds you from falling into the fire every moment.[12]

Sermons and books that emphasize God's holiness and wrath against human wickedness fall into what's informally known as "worm theology." A pillar of Calvinism, total depravity also shows up in the teaching of early-twentieth-century fire-and-brimstone evangelists. You can find versions of it in the fundamentalist Baptist teaching of the 1950s, and it became more mainstream due to the Young Restless and Reformed movement of the late twentieth century. Nondenominational and megachurch pastors like Mark Driscoll preach their own version of tough-love, hellfire-and-brimstone sermons for modern audiences. Like Edwards, these pastor-teachers claim that God's love is magnified by a hyperfocus on how humans offend God and are incapable of any good on their own. Christians operating from within this paradigm naturally believe all children, regardless of age, are sinners with depraved intent.

We heard from many people that these teachings impacted their sense of well-being and perspective about God, saddling them with a heavy burden of self-doubt and self-hatred. One respondent said,

> These teachings taught me that I was bad and that I was utterly disgusting to God unless I obeyed him.
>
> —anonymous

The Sin of Defying Godlike Parents

When parents interpret undesirable behaviors using sin categories, a perceived bad attitude or not sharing a toy might be a sin. A one-year-old squirming to be put down might be "enough to make you believe the Devil started out as an infant. . . . It causes one to understand where the concept of a 'sinful nature' originated."[13] Indeed, "rebellion can be something as simple as a small child struggling against a diaper change or stiffening his body when you want him to sit on your lap."[14] But the cardinal sin children can commit is disobeying their parents. This approach places undue emphasis on children as sinners while also viewing parents as themselves sinless authorities who possess infallible insight into the heart of another human being.

> The worst motivation was always assumed of me. There was very little room for something to be just a mistake, or unintentional. Everything was always a "heart issue," with spiritual motives and implications. . . . Everything "wrong" was a guilt trip, and we had to agree to whatever the parent said we did wrong and apologize or we would stay "in trouble." Trying to explain or having a different viewpoint was not often tolerated.
>
> —Laura

It's worth noting that the Bible verse "Obey your parents in the Lord, for this is right" (Eph. 6:1) is addressed to *children*. It does not read, "Parents, *make* your children obey." When parents interpret it that way, they may determine that it's their job to punish sin. Even though theological lip service is given about *everyone* falling short, in the family system children become sinners offending capricious whims of godlike parents. Tedd Tripp recommends that parents "unmask their child's sin" as they seek to shepherd the child's heart: "You must learn to work from the behavior you see, back to the heart. . . . Help them see the ways that they are trying to slake their souls' thirst with that which cannot satisfy."[15]

In this framework, to defy a parent is to defy God. As Tripp writes, "It is God who is not being obeyed when you are disobeyed. It is God who is not being honored when you are not honored."[16] Here, parents are in essence called to take on the role of the Holy Spirit, scrutinizing a child's motives and rendering judgment.

> Disobedience was one of the worst sins, and it was defined mostly as anything that Mom didn't like or that annoyed her (and, of course, the usual definitions of not doing things the first time, right away, cheerfully, etc.). Talking about sin was done regularly and with many Bible verses attached so we would know just how badly our existence annoyed God.
>
> —Annika

Sometimes parenting experts sell useful tools to assist with linking certain behaviors to Scripture.[17] Ginger Hubbard, who based her ministry on Tripp's teaching,[18] developed a "Wise Words for Moms" chart, a nouthetic / biblical counseling resource parents could use to discipline behaviors such as bad friendships, complaining, coveting, defiant attitude or looks, not receiving instruction, and worry.[19] For each behavior, Hubbard provides "heart probing" questions, a reproof (put off), an encouragement (put on), and additional Bible verses. For instance, if a child whines, they might be asked, "Are you communicating with a self-controlled voice? How does God want you to communicate?" Whining, according to the chart, is defined as "an ungodly form of communication," with a reference to Titus 2:12a, which instructs Christians to "say 'No' to ungodliness and worldly passions"; the chart's antidote for this is self-control, the explanation being that "God wants you to use self control, even with your voice."[20] This is followed with a reference to Titus 2:12b, "and to live self-controlled, upright and godly lives in this present age."[21]

This may seem rather innocuous—after all, plenty of parenting resources, both secular and religious, discuss self-control and whining. But is it accurate to splice up a single verse and apply it to a parenting moment, effectively equating whining with "ungodliness and worldly passions"? Is that what the passage is saying? Is whining a *sin*? How do we factor in things like a child's tiredness, hunger, or overstimulation? Children, like adults, have physical and mental limits, but they don't have a way to name or work through them in calm ways.

Hubbard thinks these considerations are excuses. She describes witnessing a mom ask her child why he had hit another child. Hubbard tells readers that she wanted to "butt in and say, 'Because he's a sinner. Why wouldn't he act like that?'" Later, Hubbard overhears the mother say that her son was napless, tired, and hungry. Hubbard thinks to herself, "Well, I'm tired and hungry, too, but I'm not going to slap you upside the head!'" In doing so, she fails to consider that children may view the world and respond in ways that do not directly mirror adult thought processes. As a result, she assigns the boy the internal monologue and expected self-restraint an adult might show. She acknowledges that tiredness may impact a child's behavior but ultimately concludes, "Sin is sin and wrong is wrong. . . . There is nothing in the Scriptures to validate the neglect of training because the child is tired or hungry. They sin, not because they are tired, hungry, or having a bad hair day, but because they are sinners."[22] An ordinary parenting moment (stop hitting your sibling) becomes imbued with theological motivations (children hit because they are sinners, and there is no excuse for sin). This reveals a unique kind of eisegesis, or reading one's own already established ideas into specific verses. A preconceived understanding of sin leads to the selection of single Bible verses as grounds for godly parents to expect sinless perfection from their children.

> I remember when I was probably three or four my mom sat me on the kitchen counter after I'd done something wrong and asked me, "How do you think that makes Jesus feel?" And that is my very first memory of feeling like I was disappointing God. It turned my normal childlike behavior, impulses, and struggles in growing up into a mindset that I had to earn God's love and affection. That, paired with other doctrine I picked up, let me know I had to get

> right, and if I didn't I was going straight to hell. There was corporal punishment used in my house, but I don't remember that as much, and I don't feel like it impacted me as much as the idea that I was consistently disappointing God. It led to suicidal ideation, a severe eating disorder, and the idea that any struggle was God's favor being removed from my life, because I had screwed up again.
>
> —Kayla

Sinful or Developmentally Appropriate?

Many Christian parenting resources allude to 1 Samuel 15:23: "For rebellion is as the sin of witchcraft, and stubbornness is as iniquity and idolatry" (KJV). This verse comes in the middle of a narrative in which Samuel the prophet is rebuking Saul, Israel's first king, whose repeated rebellion culminates in this confrontation. In response to Samuel, Saul hedges, implying that he made rebellious choices so that he could *better* worship the Lord. Much could be said about this passage, but we want to note a couple of points:

1. This passage is about a *king*, the most powerful person in the nation of Israel.
2. This king has repeatedly ignored his kingly duties, as well as direct instructions from the Lord, and instead has acted out of self-interest.
3. This king has offered deceptive and cowardly excuses to a prophet of God.
4. This king had repeated chances to change his ways and attempt a different path.

This is the context in which Samuel speaks, announcing that the kingdom will be taken from Saul and given to another. Forcing a multilayered passage describing a pivotal moment in the sweeping drama of Israel's history into a single-verse instruction about children's disobedience, as many Christian parenting pastor-teachers do, takes a narrative concept and makes it prescriptive. Applying it to a parent-child relationship distorts both the passage and that relationship. Such a misinterpretation requires readers to do the following:

1. Take a prophetic critique of a *king* and apply it to a powerless *child*.
2. Equate the direct and repeated instructions given to an *adult* by *God* with instructions given to a *child in formation* by a *parent*.
3. Take a rebuke for a repeated pattern of unethical and exploitative kingly power and apply it to a child's behavior.
4. Bolster ideas about instant obedience with a passage that describes repeated chances.

We hope it's clear that this kind of hermeneutic inverts the meaning of the text, selectively using the Bible to support something that may not even be particularly "biblical" to begin with.

When Christian parents quote 1 Samuel 15:23 at children in various stages of development, what are the implications? What does a child learn from this? That their tantrum, their resistance to bedtime, their difficulty leaving a playdate, their normal childish behavior or immature misbehavior is equivalent to witchcraft and idolatry? Is this a responsible use of Scripture?

In *Shepherding a Child's Heart*, Tedd Tripp commonly depicts children as adults in little bodies who have sinful motivations: First-grader Harold is a "relationship junkie" with "sexually loaded" thoughts; second grader George is "wicked" in spite of being well-behaved, like "one whose cup is washed and clean on the outside, but is filthy on the inside"; Genny is "overbearing" in her desire to choose certain games at recess and needs to be "rescued from a life of finding comfort and meaning in controlling others."[23] Tripp's antidote for these things is scrupulous religiosity well beyond a young child's capacity. Harold "must understand that only God can slake the thirst of his soul for relationship"; George needs to learn that "even his good behavior require[s] repentance, because . . . it reflected pride and self-righteousness"; and Genny will be taught to regularly pray to counteract her teacher-identified "overbearing" behavior.[24]

Tripp's claims regarding sin hang on his understanding of Romans 1:18–19: "The wrath of God is being revealed from heaven against all the godlessness and wickedness of men, who suppress the truth by their wickedness, since what may be known about God is plain to them, because God has made it plain to them." Tripp proof texts this in an introductory chapter titled "Your Child's Development: Godward Orientation." No commentary is offered, nor is there any attempt to meaningfully discuss this excerpt from Romans, even though it is foundational for all that follows.

Can a preverbal or young child or even a teenager understand what "God has made plain to them"? And what is that anyway? Did Paul, who is addressing new Christian converts in the early church in Rome, envision children as among the "men who suppress the truth by wickedness," and, if so, how? Tripp's book has circulated for decades as authoritatively "biblical" even though very little biblical substantiation is provided. Outside of a handful of quoted passages, most biblical references are mentioned only in passing parentheticals that are then tallied in an appendix unmoored from the rest of the book. Spiritual rhetoric veils the reality that resources can include many Bible verses and still be biblically and theologically impoverished.

The Sin of Biblical Ignorance

So, what *does* the Bible have to say about sin? And how might that relate to parenting? The Bible uses many metaphors for sin: a stain, a disease, a burden to be borne, a debt to be paid. Under the sacrificial system of Moses's day, sin was seen as something that needed to be taken outside the camp, removed from God's holy presence. Sin could pollute the body, intentionally or unintentionally, and morally corrupt the land. Sin required purification.

Elsewhere in Scripture, sin is described as a debt owed, as something bought back through a kinsman redeemer—in economic terms involving Sabbath, Jubilee, and justice. Paul frequently writes about sin as a power: a force in the world, often paired with the last enemy, death. But do such ideas show up in discussions of sin in Christian parenting teaching? If so, we certainly haven't come across them. Sometimes Christian parenting books point to judgments like the exile of the nation of Israel as evidence of God "disciplining" his children for sins, but is even this a complete picture?

According to theologian Andrew Remington Rillera, the prophets describe the exile as occurring because the land needed rest from the moral failings of Israel. This aligns with how Cornelius Plantinga Jr. writes about sin as "the spoiling of shalom, whether physically (e.g., by disease), morally, spiritually, or otherwise. Moral and spiritual evil are agential evil—that is, evil that, roughly speaking, only persons can do or have. Agential evil thus comprises evil acts and dispositions."[25] Death, powers, debt, stain, corruption are not the way it's supposed to be. This is how Plantinga sums up sin's shattering of well-being and shalom. Sin creates an impaired connection between human beings and God, self, and others. Tidy definitions for sin given from pulpits about "missing the mark" or "separation from God" aren't untrue, but they skip over the complexity found within Scripture as well as within the human condition. And these rich biblical motifs are also entirely absent from the concepts of atonement that undergird Christian parenting frameworks.

The Sin That Sent Jesus to the Cross

Most churchgoing people have heard the message that Jesus died for our sins. Sometimes this comes with illustrations like the bridge diagram, which depicts the cross closing the chasm of our sin that separates individuals from God. People are told that Jesus takes their place so that they don't have to die, or that Jesus is a sacrifice for sin. Many children (and parents) are introduced to Christian theology with the *Wordless Book*, a staple of children's ministries that is attributed to Charles Spurgeon and evolved through the efforts of Hudson Taylor and Dwight Moody. This collection of blank, colored pages is intended to help children and potential converts learn and remember a simplified "gospel message": Black is for the *sin* we all have that separates us from God. Red is for the *blood* Jesus shed to save us. White is for being washed clean and *saved*. Green is for the growth of *sanctification* that comes as a Christian. And yellow is for the golden roads of *heaven*. Perhaps you've seen this replicated in Sunday school or vacation Bible school classes where children make brightly colored beaded bracelets so they can wear this reminder on their wrists.

Overt messaging about "what Jesus did for you" pairs with the targeted spiritual instruction going on at home via Christian parenting approaches.

> I feel like sin was taught as the core of our identity. My parents were even hesitant to say that God heard us when we prayed (as children) because we were still unsaved sinners. The knowledge that even my righteousness was like filthy rags was a distinct and

> early understanding for me. I was very much taught that Jesus had died for my sins and that he wanted to save me. But the emphasis on obedience to the law and our sinful nature was heavy. As I grew older, a continual cloud of guilt and shame seemed to be at the core of who I was. As a young person, I began to exhibit signs of scrupulosity or religious OCD, though I would not have the words for it until I was much, much older. I feared that I had committed the unpardonable sin. I would go through phases where I would feel the need to apologize for the slightest thing, and I would search my motives to see if I could write the word "love" at the end of a letter to someone I genuinely cared about. As I grew older, intrusive thoughts started to come in and, with them, confusion and guilt.
>
> —anonymous

"Look for and seize the many daily opportunities you will have for highlighting and punctuating gospel truth in your kids' thinking," megachurch pastor John MacArthur advises.[26] Momfluencers on Instagram create reels to model for others how to saturate ordinary parenting moments with gospel language. Tedd Tripp says a fight over toys gives parents a chance to "[open] the way continually to the cross where forgiveness is found for twisted, warped, and sinful boys and girls."[27] A parent reading Tripp's words may be left asking, "What does it mean or look like to 'lead my child to the cross'?" Should I simply talk more about the cross? About atonement? About sin? About hell? If this is the case, who has equipped a parent for this kind of theological instruction? Most evangelical parents end up relying on a pastor-teacher's opinion.

This is a relatively new development. For most of church history, Christian children were baptized into the church as infants, thus securing their eternal salvation. Given rates of infant mortality, this was the primary focus for centuries. After the Council of Trent during the mid-1500s, local parishes began formally catechizing young people, often via a question-and-answer model such as the *Westminster Shorter Catechism* or through family devotions. When children came of age, they could enter through a process of discernment before being confirmed into the faith. Some mainline denominations still follow this pattern, but many American evangelicals have abandoned this kind of instruction in favor of market-driven children's ministry materials. Some second- or third-generation American evangelicals are unaware there are alternatives to consumer-driven catechesis.

Instead, evangelical parents turn to attractively packaged resources produced by individuals who have marketing skill and influence but little awareness of the breadth and depth of theology. These are given front-and-center product display space alongside parenting books authored by individuals who present their preferred theological ideas as definitive.

Sinning Children in the Hands of Angry Parents

In their book *The Faithful Parent*, Martha Peace and Stuart Scott encourage parents to teach their children about God's impending wrath: "No matter how sweet they are on the outside, [children] still have a depraved and selfish heart in need of God's grace," they write, explaining that Christ "bore our sins in his body as he took the wrath and punishment that we deserve. . . . Only the God-man, who was sinless and did not deserve to die or be punished for sin, could satisfy the Father's wrath."[28] Peace and Scott present the theory of penal substitutionary atonement as the comprehensive gospel message without noting that views on the atonement have varied widely throughout church history. For instance, early Christians favored the Example Theory: Christ, in his incarnation, provided believers with a model of what unfallen and restored humanity was like. The reformer John Calvin, a lawyer by training, utilized the metaphor of a courtroom with humanity on trial. There are other theories, such as Christus Victor, in which the powers of death and sin are nailed to the cross and vanquished, as well as motifs based on biblical themes: Passover, substitution, the blood of Christ, sacrifice, the Great High Priest, the Eucharist.[29]

It is beyond the scope of this book to make a case for or against penal substitutionary atonement, but it's worth noting that it has become the primary and often *only* way of understanding salvation for most conservative Christians.[30] Historically speaking, it is one among several perspectives. But making it *the* perspective—and then formulating ritualized discipline and spanking around it—verges on idolatry. When we insert parents in the role of representing a deity who requires pacifying, when we operate as though children must atone for their own sins amid sacraments of spanking, we have come far afield from an understanding of the gracious salvation provided by God. Because evangelical resources rely so heavily on the corporal punishment of children, we'll spend the next chapter examining it. Here, let's first consider the theological implications of pairing spanking with this sin and atonement framework:

1. Children of all ages have adult motivations to sin, and anything a parent doesn't like (misbehavior, wrongdoing, attitude, etc.) is sin.
2. Sin is dealt with at the cross, where God the father's wrath is satiated by the painful death of God the son. Parents are agents of God, expected to diagnose sin and help children understand how their sins displease God. God wants parents to deal with a child's sin by painfully punishing them and spanking them.

Theologically speaking, this framework positions parents to assume the roles of God the Holy Spirit (searching hearts and convicting children of sin), God the father (wrathful at sin and requiring punishment), and God the son (achieving restored fellowship after atoning punishment). "What?" you may be asking. That doesn't sound right. Didn't we just hear all about how children are told Jesus died for their sins? Children are indeed told that, and it's often paired with an explanation about how the cross was necessary because God's wrath at sin separated us from God. So, Jesus, the son, took the punishment for sin to satisfy the Father's wrath.

However, for reasons that no resource expounds on, God still seems to require parents to spank their children for their misbehavior and sin. We might speculate that this is because parental wrath still remains. The accompanying parenting scripts even bring "the cross" into the moment of spanking. In this respect, parents fashion God after their own image (an angry, displeased cosmic parent whose wrath will not be satiated without due punishment) and catechize children into it: body, mind, and soul.

7

SPARE THE ROD

The Corporal Punishment of Children

Do not let the crying of the child sway you from administering discipline, because you are sparing him from a greater disaster by administering the rod—it may be that you shall deliver his soul from hell. . . . Do you see how necessary it is to administer discipline? It is literally a question of life and death!

—Bruce Ray, *Withhold Not Correction*

To say, "I don't believe in spanking," is to say that God's ordained methods for child training are wrong. It's to reject God's Word. It's to say that you are wiser than God Himself.

—Ginger Hubbard, *Don't Make Me Count to Three*

Parents who do not discipline their children according to God's Word are *attempting to destroy their children*.

—Douglas Wilson, *Standing on the Promises* (emphasis original)

"Spanking" is a catch-all term for the corporal punishment of children. It refers to an adult striking a child on their clothed or bare buttocks with an open hand or an implement such as a paddle, wooden spoon, or slender tree branch. Some Christian parenting experts include switching toddlers on thighs or calves as spanking. Others recommend everything from glue sticks to plumbing line to pancake flippers as potential tools for this purpose. The majority of Christian resources assume parents will be spanking their children and present a timeline suggesting this should begin sometime in toddlerhood and, if done properly, will be phased out before puberty. However, there are Christian parenting resources that also recommend flicking or switching nursing infants or include anecdotes about spanking tweens and teenagers.

For most of American history, corporal punishment for children was the norm. Older cartoons and novels routinely depict characters being turned over an authority figure's knee and hit. Many adults can recall trips to the principal's office to get "paddled" in public school. Others were punished by babysitters or neighbors. Secular parenting experts of the early and mid-twentieth century write about spanking as a given, but that began to shift in the late twentieth century.

People like James Dobson still advocated for spanking, but in the 1980s and '90s the attachment parenting movement suggested an alternate way forward. Additionally, some social scientists began to study the impact of spanking and argued that it was ineffective and harmful.[1] The global conversation around human rights, including the rights of children, was changing, and in 1989 the United Nations put forward the Convention of the Rights of the Child, which thrust disciplinary methods onto the world stage. While the '90s and '00s saw numerous countries outlaw the corporal punishment of children, it's still legal in every US state, and twenty-three states still permit spanking in public schools.[2] Additionally, the United States remains the only UN member who has yet to ratify the Convention of the Rights of the Child, and the parental prerogative to educate and discipline their children as they see fit continues to be a closely held value for many Americans. According to a 2014 survey, about half of all American families still own up to utilizing corporal punishment, and that's without accounting for the likelihood of some parents being unwilling to self-report honestly.[3]

We suspect this statistic is much higher in evangelical families. Why? For one, because we heard from so many parents and children alike who testify to the ways spanking was normative. In addition, many Christian parenting resources state that God wants and even requires parents to spank their children. All the factors we've previously discussed—commitments to hierarchy and obedience, faulty hermeneutics and manipulation of biblical texts, misguided beliefs about sin and atonement—require enforcement. American evangelicals *for decades* have been told that disciplining means applying "the rod," in other words, spanking children. Here are some responses our survey participants provided regarding corporal punishment:

> My brother and I were spanked . . . until our "will was broken." I remember reading/hearing the advice to continue with the spanking until your child's cries change from anger/rebellion to more of a broken/sad tone. . . . One time I counted, and the number was forty-one.
>
> —anonymous

> I was spanked from as early as I can remember until age nineteen. Corporal punishment was used for everything. Everything.
>
> —Jennifer

Christian parents are some of the few today who still vocally defend spanking. Visit any Christian parenting online forum, and you will see evangelicals staunchly promoting spanking. Older evangelical resources expect that parents will spank their kids without embarrassment. Newer resources dodge the issue, either with diplomatic silence or something along the lines of "The Bible commands it, but keep it rare." Very few Christian resources directly suggest an alternative. While we knew that spanking would be something we'd need to address when we started writing this book, our research convinced us that the corporal punishment of children is still the norm in most evangelical homes. In fact, many pastor-teachers, as evidenced in the examples at the beginning of this chapter, tell parents that God *requires* them to spank their children.

Historical Perspectives on Spanking Children

For most of human history and across cultures, hitting children has been a fact of life. Ancient texts from Egypt indicate that the "stick and shame" were essential components of parenting.[4] The Romans saw children on par with slaves and women, subject to domination according to the will of the paterfamilias.[5] Pre-Enlightenment literature and historical records reveal the unchallenged assumption that parents will physically reprimand their children; however, there is also evidence that not every culture relied on punitive approaches. For instance, historian Stacy Patton argues that West African cultures treated children with gentleness and that the practice of "whupping children" in Black American families is a direct result of American chattel slavery.[6]

Similarly, the writings of Jesuit missionaries reveal that the corporal punishment of children was not practiced by the Huron people of North America. In one account, the missionaries describe a time when a drummer boy who was accompanying them lost control of his drumstick, accidentally striking a Huron, who demanded recompense. As a Frenchman prepared to whip the boy, "the Indians begged them to desist, and one of them shielded the boy, offering his own body for the beating."[7] These missionaries recorded their surprise at the nonpunitive ways the Indigenous people of Canada related to their children.

Even factoring in these differences, children have always been at the mercy of the adults in their families and communities. In this sense, children share the lot of women, enslaved people, the imprisoned, and others who are perceived as the property of more powerful groups of people. Pentecostal preacher Nickels J. Holmes, son of a Presbyterian minister, describes how his parents, who owned slaves, "used the same rod with their children that they did with their little colored slaves. They were kind to their slaves and thoughtful of their comfort and welfare, but they taught them obedience and righteousness."[8]

This idea that benevolent authority figures use corporal punishment as a means for kindly instruction is a staple of American culture, so it's unsurprising that spanking is promoted in Christian literature. It's usually presented in one of two ways. James Dobson often said that children were "asking for a spanking," spotlighting the affectionate and compliant disposition that came afterward. Dobson presented spanking primarily as a pragmatic tool, a method intended to show children who was boss and to obtain obedience. People who implement this kind of spanking often claim it is a "last resort." Parents attempt to explain that—without spanking—children might run into traffic (a favorite talking point) or touch a hot stove.[9] We are going to call this approach *utilitarian spanking*.

Reb Bradley, author of the book *Child Training Tips*, explains how he, as a young father and pastor, found Dobson's parenting books to be lacking. He says they weren't sufficiently "biblical" and relied on the questionable field of psychology.[10] For Bradley, if the Bible is authoritative, shouldn't we look there and only there for methods of discipline? This school of thought cultivates another approach to spanking, one we are going to call *liturgized spanking*, which shows up in Christian parenting literature around 1970. This term may sound esoteric, but a few of the resources we reviewed talk about a "liturgy of spanking," so it captures both the ritual and the way it's written about as carrying supreme spiritual weight.

Jay Adams writes that obeying parents is "the first commandment with a promise," one that "also implies a threat."[11] The threat of discipline, specifically corporal punishment, is something many pastor-teachers present as God-endorsed, and they looked to specific Bible verses to justify their position—primarily "the rod" verses in Proverbs and an interpretation of Hebrews 12 that saw fatherly discipline as primarily punitive (see Prov. 13:24; 22:15; 23:13; 29:15; Heb. 12:7–9). Spanking wasn't merely something *everyone* did or a tool used to enforce compliance; it became something quasi-sacred—*God's* method. As a result, it wasn't enough to mention it in passing, like many utilitarian spanking resources did; instead, as Independent Fundamentalist Baptist pastor Jack Hyles writes in *How to Rear Children*, "spanking should be a ritual."[12] We discussed some theological incentives to spank in the previous chapter, and these combine with perceived biblical grounds to sweep away any ethical concerns. If the Bible commands it, parents must do it. And as the United States began to see a strong cultural shift away from corporal punishment, Christians committed to the practice made an even stronger case for it.[13]

Soon, chapters on spanking weren't enough. Books focused solely on spanking, often authored by biblical counseling advocates, began to appear on the market: Roy Lessin's *Spanking: Why? When? How?*, Larry Tomczak's *God, the Rod, and Your Child's Bod*, and Bruce Ray's *Withhold Not Correction* were oriented primarily around discipline, which became code for "spanking."

This legacy continues today. Some Christian parents use "discipline" and "spanking" as synonyms. Journalist Anne-Marie

Cusac, author of the book *Cruel and Unusual*, suggests that the spanking manuals of the 1970s were shaped by broader social attitudes toward crime and punishment. Cusac argues that as societies become accustomed to an ends-justifies-the-means approach to physical force in certain areas—for instance, military defense, to preserve law and order, or to prevent criminal behavior—individuals are more likely to use force to achieve their own ends. This tracks with how American evangelicals began to write about spanking as an unquestionable, divinely ordained good during the years that American society in general was becoming tough on crime.

Parents were told that by employing the relatively lesser pain of spanking, children could be spared from the greater pain of being imprisoned for criminal behavior or even the eternal consequence of hell. Roy Lessin writes that sometimes multiple spankings are needed close together even if they leave marks on a child. "It is better," he concludes, "for children to carry a few temporary marks on the outside than to carry within them areas of disobedience and wrong attitudes that can leave permanent marks on their character."[14]

The idea that pain wards off depravity is clearly evident on the pages of Puritan teaching and in revivalist preaching that focused on eternal punishment and damnation. Jonathan Edwards, who wrote collections of sermons for children, contrasted beatific imagery about Christ and his love with fearsome and vivid descriptions of hell and the loss of God's affection. Given everyday realities like child mortality, plague, and how swiftly loved ones could die, avoiding damnation and securing a good afterlife became a powerful motivator. Edwards and others "instinctively knew how to exploit common childhood fears of darkness, 'monsters,' abandonment, and death."[15]

In his book *Spare the Child: The Religious Roots of Punishment and the Psychological Impact of Physical Abuse*, historian Philip Greven shares many Christian leaders' accounts of their own childhoods, including how they were punished. Oral Roberts joked, "Papa believed in the stars and stripes. He put on the stripes, and Vaden and I saw the stars. When he got us home he took down his big razor strap. It was made in two pieces. When he got through with us, we believed it had a thousand pieces."[16]

Greven's book includes many stories that Christian leaders recounted for laughs as they described their childhood punishment before thanking their parents. Adult children today similarly reflect back with commentary like "I probably deserved it" or "I'm glad my parents spanked me; I'm better for it" or jokes about misbehaving children and the need for wooden spoons and belts. Even though these adults may be well into middle age and beyond, their parents can still do no wrong, and spanking is a point of humor. David Wilkerson, author of *The Cross and the Switchblade*, describes his parents' "woodshed" therapy: "Each of us had a holy respect for Dad's razor strap that hung on a big nail on the way downstairs to the coal bin. Dad conducted all his 'counseling sessions' in that coal bin. . . . I believe it's time for a woodshed revival!"[17]

There are exceptions. Martin Luther, who was "beat by his mother until the blood ran" and "by his father until he ran away from home" and "by school masters for 'nothing at all,'" seems not to have hit his own children. "I know of nothing that would give me greater sorrow," Luther writes, concluding that striking his five-year-old son might cause the child to become shy and hate both his earthly and heavenly fathers.[18] The evangelist Dwight Moody was whipped as a boy and never repeated that practice with his own children. His son Paul, near the end of his life, recalled a moment when Dwight once spoke harshly while correcting him, something so rare it caused him to cry. "But I had barely gotten into my little bed," he recounts, "before he was kneeling beside it in tears and seeking my forgiveness for having spoken so harshly. He never, he said, intended to speak crossly to one of his children."[19]

In addition, there has always been a small minority of Christians calling for gentler practices, particularly as women advocated for children and their education. Lydia Marie Child, author of *The Mother's Book*, wrote, "I have said much in praise of gentleness. I cannot say too much. Its effects are beyond calculation."[20] Charlotte Mason, the famed British educator, taught parents and teachers to approach children with a posture of respect, using encouragement, living examples, and consequences rather than forcing compliance.[21] The Reverend Jacob Abbott, who wrote child-rearing advice books in the late 1800s, did not practice corporal punishment. His son Lyman recalls, "I do not remember that he ever punished me. Yet I not only do not recall that I ever thought of disobeying him, but I do not remember ever to have seen a child refuse him obedience."[22]

These voices have been drowned out by louder proclamations that claim Christian parents have always spanked and warn that gentler approaches will lead to progressivism and nightmare behaviors. Even in 1888, J. C. Ryle wrote of his "decided protest against the modern notion that no child ought ever to be whipped. Doubtless some parents use bodily correction far too much, and far too violently; but many others, I fear, use it too little."[23]

Christian Spanking Manuals and Liturgized Spanking

Utilitarian spanking advocates portray discipline as a means to enforce compliance, but liturgized spanking leans heavily into the idea that "God has required us to inflict pain on those dear to us."[24] Corporal punishment should be thorough because, as Ginger Hubbard explains, borrowing directly from Bruce Ray, "a good spanking at the end of the day can never make up for the spankings that should have been administered throughout the day."[25] Larry Tomczak reports to parents that "loving correction reinforces with a painful experience the principle of the parents' authority over the child, and lets the child know that the particular action or attitude is unacceptable. He is totally secure in the parent's love."[26]

These pastor-teachers don't attempt to substantiate their claims that spanking will produce godly results or make a child feel secure in a parent's love. They don't explain *why* spanking brings a child "to a point where he is more likely to receive the Word of God" and helps a parent "enjoy a close and open relationship with the child."[27] They simply reassure parents that somehow, because parents tell themselves the spankings are loving, *children will receive them as loving*. "It is amazing how peaceful and happy a child can be after they have received a good spanking," Nancy Campbell enthuses.[28]

Spanking is perceived as effective because children become "peaceful" and compliant, securing highly prized obedience. Doug Wilson promises that spanking clears the air of a "backlog of unconfessed sin." He recounts a moment when his toddler daughter was "looking for a spanking because she wanted to be clean" and, after receiving one, turned into "a ray of sunshine."[29] No consideration is given to child development or a child's perspective; instead, parents are offered anecdotes from other families as indirect promised outcomes. Bruce Ray describes how parents of an "adopted four-year-old rebel who also had physical disabilities" began spanking her consistently such that "their daughter's personality changed 99%. She began to obey them, peace entered into their home, and love was at last able to flow freely in both directions."[30]

The "rules" for how liturgized spanking is supposed to work, the defining characteristics that somehow demarcate it as "godly" (as opposed to simply hitting children into compliance), are provided in checklists generated by this crop of spanking advocates. Renaming it "chastisement" or "applying the rod" gives the ritual a special, almost sacred, weight. The manuals don't agree on a formula, but here are some common ingredients: specific instruments, pulling down their child's pants and spanking their bare bottom, and making sure to administer punishment calmly—even going to another room to pray first if needed, while children wait in expectation of impending punishment. It's impossible to say whether an angry, raging parent or a detached, prayerful one who believes they are doing God's work causes more harm. But those following the latter approach were told over and over again to be confident.

"God in his wisdom," Larry Tomczak says in a sing-song voice in his seminar titled "How to Raise Respectful, Responsible, and Obedient Children," "prepared a strategic place on our children's anatomy which has enough cushiony, fatty tissue and sensitive nerve endings to respond to Spirit-led stimulation. . . . All children come equipped with one!"[31] Many resources make a joke to this effect,[32] though a few warn about spanking only on the bottom to avoid injury to other parts of the body. Some experts indicate that children *like* being spanked. Rachel Jankovik, author of *Loving the Little Years*, explains that "spanked kids are happy kids," drawing on her own personal recollections of "affectionate" spanking.[33] Roy Lessin describes a time when his wife was in a hurry about the spanking. "When she finished [my son] turned to her and said, 'Mommy, could you spank me again? Only this time let me pull down my jeans. It didn't hurt enough.' . . . It helped us to realize how much children need *effective* discipline in order to bring them release."[34]

Parents, for their part, are trusting that if they follow the experts' often extraordinarily detailed advice, it will magically turn hitting children into God-approved spanking. Parents are to listen for the sound of a penitent cry, but not too much of a cry.[35] "Examine the way in which you spank," Ray advises. "Is it causing grief and sorrow, followed by sweet submission—the marks of biblical correction? Today that father who learned to take his son's pants down is rejoicing. . . . His son is already much more obedient."[36] Tedd Tripp recommends multiple rounds of spanking if a child isn't "sweet" afterward.[37] Lessin describes how he needed to teach his preschool daughter not to "fight the spanking" by "spank[ing] her separately for her [resistance]. . . . It was responsible for bringing a special sweetness and happiness to her entire disposition."[38] Voddie Baucham endorses "all day spanking sessions" in which parents "wear [their children] out."[39] Nancy Wilson laughs about spanking her toddler son upward of forty times for not staying in his bedroom during naptime.[40] L. Elizabeth Krueger says she had "a dozen occasions to spank [my six year old]" on the morning of "the Big Change," the day she decided to crack down on disciplinary measures.[41] Other authors encourage parents to implement what Doug Wilson calls a "Reign of Terror," wherein parents offer "no warnings, and spankings for all offenses."[42] Tripp takes a calmer, if equally disturbing approach, encouraging parents to sit their children down, apologize for slacking off, and let them know they will now be spanked in earnest.[43] "I had to make sure that when each conflict was over, I'd won," Krueger says, summing it up, "and that I'd won decidedly."[44]

This idea of "winning" shows up in many of the spanking manuals and relies on a parent accurately diagnosing a child's motives as rooted in defiance. Krueger recounts how her daughter was "clever and calculating" at age four. Told to put a book and shoes away, she put the book next to the shelf (not on it) and the shoes outside the closet door (not inside). Krueger determined that "almost obeying is not obeying at all. I hated to do it, but I woke her up, spanked her, told her flatly that she had disobeyed, and I made her 'fix' each of her little 'mistakes.'"[45] Waking up children to spank them is a surprisingly common thread in the manuals, perhaps a result of the value placed on thoroughness, winning, and taking sin seriously. Hubbard describes sending her three-year-old daughter to her room until she could tell the truth. The little girl was there long enough to fall asleep, after which her mother woke her up to give her a spanking. "[My daughter] was absolutely relieved and thankful to get a spanking. Her heart was clean," Hubbard concludes.[46]

Story after story in book after book depicts similar scenes as exemplary. Spanking isn't just something to use when a parent loses it in a frazzled moment or to secure quick compliance because a child might run into a busy street; it becomes *the* primary means of discipline, punishment, instruction, and even catechesis. "Discipline," Bruce Ray says, "can in some ways be likened to preaching a sermon."[47]

Parents are promised: If you preach the spanking sermon soundly, you will spank less and less as the child gets older. But is this the case? Some children comply to avoid punishment, but perhaps compliant children would obey even without corporal punishment.

> I don't remember a lot of the spanking because I was so young, six months to six years, when it happened. After that point, I rarely needed spanking because I had become a very obedient, passive child. . . . I learned quickly to do what I was told or else.
>
> —Serena

Other adults report that preverbal spanking did not safeguard them from further spankings as they aged. Instead, it seems, for parents who relied on spanking, they escalated their efforts as their children grew older.

> He tried not to spank in anger, . . . but there was still a lot of confusion when I heard the words "I love you" combined with pain. As I got older, I was embarrassed to pull down my pants and let my dad see my underwear. . . . My mother was more severe in her punishments. Spankings may have started as "prescribed" with us bent over a chair and smacked with a wooden spoon, but they would often go much further. She would tell us that a spanking

> was to take away our sin, and only she would know when we were truly repentant. There were some "spankings" that lasted upwards of an hour, where she hit various parts of our bodies, made us stand in various states of undress, and required other siblings to watch the ordeal.
>
> —Autumn

The manuals themselves exhaustively list proper instruments and methodology, making one wonder if *less* spanking was ever meant to be the goal. Rods, switches, glue sticks, and wooden spoons are all pitched to parents. Homespun industries like Etsy shops will even sell you a "board of education"—hand-carved wooden paddles engraved with Bible verses. Doug Wilson warns that "you might hurt your hand if you don't use a tool" but allows for selecting "a judicious application of a mini-rod to a mini-person," the idea being that nursing mothers might get away with flicking their infants if needed.[48] Martha Peace and Stuart Scott say no to a tree switch because it could tear the skin, no to a belt because it could hurt the wrong place, but yes to a proper instrument that allows a parent to get a good grip: "As the child grows bigger and stronger the . . . mother will usually need some sort of instrument for spanking."[49] Elisabeth Elliot recalls there being switches above every doorway in her childhood home.[50] Michael and Debi Pearl recommend cutting one's own switch or relying on plumbing line.[51] Gwen Shamblin suggests glue sticks because "it really hurts, but it doesn't leave marks on your children."[52] Parents obeyed.

> Our oldest . . . would be hit with a thin piece of pvc piping . . . until her very strong spirit relented and she stopped crying in pain. We left bruises. I left bruises. It was me most of the time inflicting this on her tiny body for the smallest and stupidest of "reasons" . . . starting when she was a toddler. . . . She is grown and a mother

herself now and is still impacted and impeded by the way we "trained" her as a toddler / small child.

—anonymous

Experts told parents that pain was an indicator of love; in turn, parents repeated this to their kids. A popular sermon illustration of a shepherd breaking a naughty sheep's leg in order to teach the sheep to stop straying circulated and stayed in many people's memories. The sheep story has been debunked numerous times.[53] One real-life shepherd even remarked that hitting sheep would cause them to run away in fear, and that this would make the job of shepherding harder. It would both erode the trust of the hit sheep and spook the watching flock. Even still, the sentiment remains: There is something good and necessary about hurting and causing bodily harm in order to control and produce a desired outcome.

Because Christian parents were told the Bible *requires* them to spank, they were impervious to the growing body of evidence that spanking increases aggression and antisocial behavior and results in trauma. Parenting experts doubled down with the simple rationale that God commands it: "The use of the rod is an act of faith. God has mandated its use. The parent obeys, not because he perfectly understands how it works, but because God has commanded it."[54] John Piper claimed that he would rather go to jail than give up his right to spank his child.[55] This brash insistence, and the fact that so many evangelical pastor-teachers were speaking in unison, misled parents to believe that pushback against spanking must be religious persecution. Furthermore, they were told that if they followed the biblical way, there could be no real danger. In fact, parents were told that the danger was *not* to spank, and it was up to them to make sure they took the advice contained in these manuals and figured out a way to apply it. This dangerously left it to parents to determine tools, intensity, regularity, and escalation—all behind closed doors and with no oversight or accountability.

Pastor-teachers advised parents not to spank in public so as to avoid a visit from Child Protective Services. This, perhaps more than anything else, hints that Christian experts were well aware that their methods were questionable. But they still clearly and repeatedly recommended parents take measures to avoid external scrutiny and accountability for what was ultimately a subjective practice. It was up to parents to determine for what and for how long and to what extent spanking was administered. This is one reason why there's such a range of practices and impact—even among our survey respondents. What happened in Christian homes was known only to parents and children.

> My parents were encouraged to start spanking their children when they were six months old. . . . When I was smaller, Mom would make me bend over her knee so she could trap my legs between hers and restrain me during spanking sessions. . . . At thirteen I had a woman's body and towered over her, so Mom relied on fear to keep me motionless. . . . My body felt violated every time I was spanked.
>
> —Diana

When parents have complete, unchecked authority, when they are told not only that they should rely on corporal punishment but also that God requires them to administer it, when they are empowered by manuals that matter-of-factly recommend implements to secure penitent cries and weed out sin, it is a recipe for child abuse. Please do not skim past that. *Popular Christian parenting teaching has enabled and exacerbated child abuse.* In our view, it's impossible to read Christian spanking manuals one after another and come to any other conclusion.

Spanking and Child Abuse

Abuse is the true legacy of spanking. Historian Philip Greven devotes a section of his book *Spare the Child* to documenting the ways children are impacted by spanking meted out in an authoritarian religious home: anxiety, hate, diminished empathy, apathy, depression, suicidality, obsessiveness, ambivalence toward parents, dissociation, paranoia, sadomasochism, domestic violence, aggression, delinquency, authoritarianism, and apocalyptic impulses.[56] Listening to the recollections of adult children is especially important, because it's difficult to conduct research into spanking. All data is self-reported, relies on memory, and cannot factor in mitigating factors or the subjectivity of spanking practices, let alone the chicken-and-the-egg dynamic. (Are abusive people more likely to opt for spanking, or does spanking train parents to be abusive?)

Still, a number of studies over the past sixty years have considered different aspects of the effects of corporal punishment. Elizabeth Gershoff, who has devoted her life to this work, conducted a meta-analysis of decades of research and found "[spanking was] linked to more aggression, more delinquent behavior, more mental health problems, worse relationships with parents, and putting the children at higher risk for physical abuse from their parents." When asked by people why she didn't look for the benefits of spanking, Gershoff replied, "We did, and there were none. We see consistently that the more children are spanked, the more behavioral problems they have in the years ahead."[57]

Other historians and scholars—for example, Janet Heimlich in her book *Breaking Their Will: Shedding Light on Religious Child Maltreatment* and Alice Miller in her book *For Your Own Good: Hidden Cruelty in Child-Rearing and the Roots of Violence*—have written extensively about how religious spanking practices are a form of physical, emotional, and sexual abuse with long-lasting implications. Unfortunately, this evidence is often disregarded by devout parents, who instead choose to believe that "the rod is somewhat of a mystery in how it works but we can be confident that while we are obeying God and working on the buttocks, God is honoring our obedience and working on the heart."[58] These parents must first be persuaded that the Bible does not, in fact, require Christian parents to "spank" their children.

We were relieved to discover that several popular evangelical Christian experts have spoken out against spanking. Given the lopsided nature of Christian parenting resources and the pushback we have witnessed in conversations around this topic, this probably was a difficult and costly thing to do. Clay Clarkson, in his book *Heartfelt Discipline*, describes how he and his wife Sally, popular speakers in Christian homeschooling circles, chose not to spank any of their children, and he makes a biblical case against spanking.[59] L. R. Knost released her book, *Jesus, the Gentle Parent*, in 2014, critiquing many Christian parenting approaches and making a robust biblical case for an attachment-oriented version of Christian parenting. William Sears, a Christian pediatrician, popularized attachment parenting principles among wider mainstream audiences.

In recent years, Christian influencers and online platforms such as Flourishing Homes and Families have advocated for gentler approaches and developed content to debunk the idea that spanking is biblical. Even John Rosemond, a Dobson-esque "common sense" biblical parenting expert, rightly points out that "nowhere in the whole of Scripture does God prescribe a specific form of discipline for children."[60] Jim and Lynne Jackson, who began their parenting ministry, Connected Families, in 2002, encourage parents to reconsider spanking and instead ask, "What is the message my children are getting from spanking? Is that the one I want? Am I safe [for] them or am I not?"[61]

Other Christian experts attempt a middle-of-the-road approach. "If I say, 'I don't spank,' I've immediately lost half the audience," influencer Abbie Halberstadt explains in a podcast episode in which she argues that gentle parenting is unbiblical. "If I say, 'I do spank,' I've lost the other half."[62] Karis Kimmel Murray responds to parents who ask her whether they should spank by telling them, "If you're a grace-based parent raising your kids in a grace-based culture, whether you choose to spank or not is up to you, and *I don't care*."[63] To our knowledge, the 2024 book *The Flourishing Family: A Jesus-Centered Guide to Parenting with Peace and Purpose*, by David and Amanda Erickson, is the first traditionally published evangelical parenting book to clearly make a robust biblical and research-based case against spanking.

It's impossible to know how many Christian parents today are spanking their children or applying other punitive measures like withholding food, locking them in their rooms, or making up religious-themed punishments like "play fasts," where children can play only on Sundays. We decided to place this chapter near the end of the book because we hope that all the previous chapters will help readers understand *why* spanking has such a stranglehold on the Christian community: commitments to biblical authority, interpretations of Scripture that promise practical results, pressure for well-behaved children, beliefs about sin and a parent's uncontested authority. All these strands weave a tight net around Christian families. This is why on this topic we are going to depart from simply providing information and offer parenting advice: *Christian parents, please stop spanking your children in God's name. The Bible does not require you to spank.*[64] We hope hearing this frees you enough to examine the research that shows the harm that spanking does and to listen to the adult children who name ways practices of spanking hurt them.

It's possible a parent might spank and end up with a child who says, "I was spanked, and I turned out fine." We've spoken to people who truthfully attest to that, but that's the best-case scenario for a not particularly effective method of control. Given that many other adults list a host of harms and negative effects that followed them into adulthood, is it really worth the gamble?

We Never Intended That

Reb Bradley, pastor and author of *Child Training Tips: What I Wish I Had Known When My Children Were Young* (1995), told us how he, as a young parent, studied the Bible to produce a diagnostic tool for parents.[65] He also relied on the commonsense teaching of his good friend J. Richard Fugate, author of *What the Bible Says About Child Training*. Bradley and Fugate both believed that the Bible served as an instruction manual for parenting and that no additional expertise was needed. Bradley taught Fugate's parenting methods to his growing church of several hundred people three times a year for many years. He also applied these principles to his own parenting.

However, when his children became adults, Bradley realized that the principles hadn't *worked*. By his account, exerting more control only resulted in broken relationships and more rebellion. He recalled a fruitless session of spanking a sixteen-year-old and in hindsight saw the need for a more functional alternative, a way that took *relationship* into account. This, Bradley told us, wasn't something he had considered before, even though he had penned a parenting manual that had sold over one hundred thousand copies due to his regular speaking gigs at homeschooling conferences in the '90s and '00s.

"I never intended for you to do that," Fugate said when Bradley explained the problems he was having with his young adult children. Bradley claims to have later amended his resources to include a more relational element, something he first learned about, he said, from Michael Pearl.[66] This, to anyone who has heard of the Pearls, may come as something of a surprise. Michael and Debi Pearl, self-styled Christian parenting experts, are infamous for their self-published parenting manual *To Train Up a Child*, which introduces the concept of "blanket training." Crawling infants are placed on blankets, tempted off them with a toy, and then switched back into place until they learn to read parental facial expressions and obey every wish and command. Pearl fashioned his disciplinary methods after principles he claims he learned from Amish horse trainers. While the Pearls' reach is unclear (their website states "Over a million copies sold!"), their work has become synonymous with child abuse in many circles.

Sean Paddock,[67] Lydia Schatz,[68] and Hana-Grace Rose Williams[69] are three children whose parents killed them while implementing Michael and Debi Pearls' parenting advice. The prosecuting attorney in one case and the physician who offered expert testimony in another named the Pearls' books as key ingredients to these tragic outcomes.[70] Still, the Pearls continue to defend their teachings.[71] Bradley told us how he had spoken with Michael Pearl on the phone about one of the families and visited one of the couples, former church members of his, in prison after they had been charged with second-degree murder, torture, and voluntary manslaughter and corporal injury of their seven-year-old child. When we asked Bradley whether this tragic outcome made him rethink his position on corporal punishment or whether he thought Michael had reconsidered his own teaching, Bradley's answer was "We never intended for them to do that. . . . Spanking for five, even ten minutes is too much, let alone two hours."[72]

What are we to make of this? Is this a sufficient answer for the countless adult children we heard from who detail egregious abuse and trauma? For the brokenhearted and angry parents who write us things like "Ruined my one chance at motherhood. Picking up the pieces now—with my grown children—and ever will be. Lost my 34-year marriage too—because I refused to submit to this sickness anymore"?[73] For Sean, Lydia, Hana-Grace, and the countless invisible children who suffer in Christian homes?

Some spanking holdouts may be tempted to say, "Well, that's Michael *Pearl*. His teaching is *fringe*. Reb Bradley was popular with homeschooling families. These aren't mainstream teachers." While Bradley and Pearl *are* household names in certain circles, we want to make sure to underscore our point with a gold-standard Christian parenting name: Tedd Tripp, whose book *Shepherding a Child's Heart* was one of the most popular Christian parenting books of the twentieth century.

The first part of Tripp's book outlines his belief that parents need to act as God's agents of authority and are therefore responsible for diagnosing their children's sin and punishing them accordingly. The second part of the book lays out seven steps for spanking children. Ginger Hubbard, who wrote the practical application companion manual, also relies on Tripp's methodology. Together they have reached (and continue to reach) millions of families in America and globally.

As we were writing this book, we learned of a new headline. Jonathan S. Russell, a church volunteer in Saginaw, Michigan, had been caught spanking young boys. It wasn't the first time. Years before, he had done time for abusing boys on the Little League team he coached. As part of his defense, he brought a copy of Tripp's book to the courtroom. "If you fail to spank, you don't take God seriously and don't love your child enough," Russell read from the book. He went on to say, regarding his own behavior, "I recognize the misapplication in the sense that these weren't my children, and this wasn't my place."[74]

This situation reveals an uncomfortable truth. A criminal court charged Russell with "two counts of second-degree criminal sexual conduct with a victim 13 or younger, four counts of assault and battery, and single counts of second-degree sexual assault, second-degree child abuse, indecent exposure, and accosting children for immoral purposes."[75] These are behaviors that would get anyone assault charges if done to another adult or swift allegations of abuse if someone else did it to your child, yet these are the behaviors Tripp and others confidently teach are God's way. How hollow might that ring in the ears of Russell's victims, who now carry the burden of trauma, or the countless children who continue to untangle the painful lessons they learned over a parent's knee?

Tripp didn't respond to our interview request, but I wonder what he would say if he had. Would he, like others, deny culpability? *But of course I didn't intend for anyone to do that!* Intent doesn't mitigate impact, and we are not interested in short-circuiting an honest reckoning of the harm and injury that countless children have endured in the name of God. With that in mind, it's time to discuss the *impact* of these teachings.

Part 3

Where Do We Go from Here?

Letting Go of the Myths and Finding Freedom

8

THE RECEIPT COMES DUE

False Promises and Betrayed Families

It's time to ask, "What was the fruit of all this?"

It's hard to quantitatively assess the fallout of family-life teaching. In studies evaluating the impact of specific practices, such as spanking, researchers are limited in the scope of their research. This is because the task is monumental. Research involving children raises serious ethical concerns; for example, there's no way to plan a study in which one group gets spanked and another does not. Research considers *self-reported* behaviors and impact, but shame, family loyalty, the subjectivity of memory, and myriad other things naturally affect findings. If researchers responsibly get through all of that, they still must make a determination: How do we quantify subjective practices and account for elements respondents may not be equipped to name or identify?

For instance, peer-reviewed research on the corporal punishment of children demonstrates that spanking is associated with increased aggression and statistically significant negative outcomes[1] and is not measurably more effective than nonviolent methods.[2] But you can also find research claiming spanking doesn't have more observable negative effects than other methods.[3] And there's also evidence it causes the kind of trauma response in children's brains that more severe forms of mistreatment do.[4] Peer-reviewed research can help identify trends, but it cannot "prove" or "quantify" impact.

The way popular Christian family-life teaching impacted *individuals* within families varies as much as the individual family dynamics do. Things like cultural context, ways parents exacerbated or mitigated dynamics, and the influence of surrounding communities all contribute to someone's unique experience. Even siblings from within the same family can report differing experiences. Attempting to identify one-size-fits-all results would be dishonest and misleading, so we aim to do two things in the following section: (1) share the responses of people describing the impact in their own words and (2) share general observations about outcomes.

Interview Responses

As we researched primary source teaching, we invited adult children and parents to tell us their stories. Representative selections from our survey responses in this book exemplify how this played out for many families. We also invite you to consider how you and the people in your family or community would describe outcomes, impact, and childhood experiences.

Some who grew up in "Dobson households" told us about the strained relationships they now have with their parents and the pain that comes alongside reexamining their childhood. They felt that love was conditional, earned by their obedience and good-naturedness. We heard from people who remember being afraid of their parents and who wish they could undo the relational damage and enjoy friendship with them later in life. Here is a sampling of those responses:

> My parents were heavily influenced by Dr. Dobson and techniques and concepts from *Shepherding a Child's Heart* and *To Train Up a Child*. . . . Two of my core beliefs as a child were that I was under authority and didn't have the right to make choices and decisions about my life, and that God and my parents would only love and protect me if I obeyed. . . . Intentionally or not, my parents taught me that their love was conditional and behavior-based, and since they represented God to me, I also grew up believing that God's love for me was conditional. . . . My husband and I are not close with our parents. It seems that once the authority was lifted (when we got married in our early twenties), there was nothing left to sustain a relationship. My parents are mostly absent from our lives and the lives of their grandchildren. . . .
>
> I wish I could be friends with my parents. I wish that they had spent my childhood getting to know me and making me feel loved instead of maintaining the status quo. I wish I felt safe with them. I wish I didn't have a panic attack when I have to confront them about something minor. I wish I didn't feel like a perpetual child in their presence. All I have wanted in my entire life is to be loved by them, and the ache has only gotten more intense as I have had my own children and struggled with how in the world they could've possibly cared so little about me as a person. I look in the faces of my children, and all I want is for them to know how loved and important they are—by God and by their parents. I deserved that too.
>
> —anonymous

> I understand now that my parents were young and inexperienced and also very excited and caught up in the Jesus movement. . . . So they were doing what they thought was best, but I am still a little salty about that.

As a kid, I remember my grandma making occasional snarky comments about how she took all her kids to Sunday school but then as adults they "got saved and found God." I thought it was sour grapes then, but now that I have moved two thousand miles away from my family and practice (or don't) religion on my own terms, I sympathize with her. Recently my mom said that her biggest regret is not urging her children to forge personal relationships with God. That shocked me, because our whole childhoods were enmeshed with the church and constantly hearing about the importance of our relationship with God.

Our family does not talk about religion or politics when we get together, but I sense that all but one sibling (who attends a megachurch) has grappled with the faith style in which we were brought up.

—Carmen

My parents and I are not as close as we were when I was growing up. . . . There are many things now that we can no longer have conversations about.

I wish my parents had had more community around them as they were raising us. We moved every couple years during my early childhood, and it was somewhat isolating. Nobody really saw me grow up except my parents and sister. I wish they could have been given language to communicate when they were upset without yelling, or that they would have learned to give a person space when they were angry instead of heaping shame on them.

—anonymous

I wish my parents could understand how terrified I was of them and how I felt like they hated me (while also loving me . . . it was confusing) and how their parenting set me up to be in an abusive marriage.

I have a very shallow yet good relationship with my parents and two out of three of my siblings. One sibling has very little to do with the rest of the family. I have a good relationship with

> my remaining living set of grandparents, although that has been strained at times over things I did they viewed as sinful (nose piercing and tattoos). What I wish was different is the ability to be completely myself with my family. There is much they don't know about me because I can't be authentic. I am raising my kids to be themselves without fear of repercussions. I give them free rein to tell me when I have hurt them and to give me a chance for reparations. They are allowed to simply be.
>
> —Jennifer

We also heard from parents who expressed deep regret and sorrow, sharing that they spanked their children because they believed they were doing the right, godly thing. Looking back, they wish that they had been given other tools to connect with their children rather than feeling they had to defend parental authority at all costs. They believed the advice that was presented to them as "biblical"—and reinforced by friends, family, and fellow church members—reflected God's will for them and their children.

> My father-in-law loves to tell the story of getting the belt when he did wrong, and how he would get an extra one every day after school for "any sin his parents didn't know about." . . . He speaks about it positively. Both sets of parents want us to have a tighter rein on our son's behavior, but it is things like crying or showing anger. I still can't show emotions without feeling shame, and I refuse to instill that in my own son.
>
> As a young mom, I spanked our child. Over and over we had been told it was the only discipline that God approved of. It made me sick. I'd spank my child and then go weep by myself. Thank God for Christian friends who spoke openly about other discipline strategies and bore with my self-righteous insistence that I must continue in my way. I began to research the early childhood development effects of spanking and praying about it. I became convicted that the purpose of my parenting is to

model God to my child. God has never "spanked" me even in my rankest sin.

—Kristin

My perspective is that of a mother who inflicted these punishments on my children, the greatest amount of it by far on our precious oldest, and although I have done over a decade of work in therapy and other healing practices, recalling those years still brings tears to my eyes almost instantly and the shame can still be stirred if I poke it even a bit. Goodness, the tears are streaming seeing this in black and white.

I do have hope, though. I have a close relationship with all four of my kids, even if it is often fraught with my oldest. In everything I lost, I have what I wanted most and that is them. We have started to rebuild, the five of us, and now six again with my granddaughter, and I see good and joy in our future.

—anonymous

Some of the people we heard from reflected on the ways their parents' practice of "good Christian parenting" distorted their view of God. Some are still trying to restore the marred picture of God they received, to understand him as a loving father rather than a mercurial, exacting judge.

We were definitely raised with the idea that we were depraved to the core, that God loved us in spite of anything about ourselves, and that hell was our birthright. I was terrified that I might not be a Christian and be bound for eternal conscious torment. I remember that Mom told me once that when she was young, she thought she was a Christian but wasn't, and that always scared me.

I was told that if I doubted total depravity, parenthood would make me certain of it. Now, as a parent, the opposite is true, and it makes me really sad that this was the view of kids in the worldview I was raised in. I see so much goodness in my children. . . . As a parent, I have removed ALL threats from how I talk about Jesus and relating to God.

—anonymous

Observations from Outside the United States

We wrote this book with White American evangelicals in mind because the most popular Christian parenting resources were produced by White American evangelicals; however, these ideas were also exported via American missionaries and ministries that expanded internationally. Rebekah Mui, founding editor of *The Kingdom Outpost*,[5] notes that the cultural respect for elders in traditional settings served the interests of globally expanding ministries. For example, when Bill Gothard, whose international seminars Mui's family attended, insisted there was something inherently feminine and Christian about women rejecting pants, Malaysian Christians wore skirts to the conference out of deference to the leader—but not in acceptance of the teaching. Malaysian Christians didn't perceive, as Gothard did, that *pants* were inherently a symbol of feminism; in fact, pants are part of traditional Malaysian clothing for women.

While Christian empire builders exported the culture war in various ways, much was lost in translation across geographic lines and came with unique cross-cultural impacts. Mui described hearing James Dobson's Focus on the Family radio devotionals, presented as authoritative teaching from an expert psychologist, as she shopped at her local grocery store in Malaysia. This masking of the political motivations of American pastor-teachers combined with preexisting colonial missionary patterns and resulted in popular *American evangelical* family teaching being presented without qualification as universal *Christian* family teaching.

We also heard from European Christians who described how shocking it was that American Christians spanked their children. In many European countries, spanking is illegal,[6] and Christians who spank are the anomaly. Those who do spank typically cite American pastor-teachers as their guide. This is a topic worthy of further exploration, particularly when one considers how teaching in these books may blend with cultural complexity. Prudy Ray, a Dalit ex-Christian, told us that American evangelical ideas about family hierarchy have contributed to preexisting cultural patriarchy and discrimination in India. While all marginalized groups face caste oppression, women are also oppressed by patriarchy from both Hinduism and Christianity, Ray said.[7] Instead of helping new converts break free of destructive cycles, exported American Christian teachings on "headship," "complementarianism," and "submission" enable ongoing abuse. And while some of these resources from the '90s and '00s may feel "old" to American audiences, we heard from a Mexican children's minister describing how resources like Tripp's and Dobson's are still popular and even gaining popularity in some areas. Reb Bradley indicated this as well, explaining that while he has retired from his dwindling domestic speaking engagements, he still travels to Korea to speak at homeschooling conferences there.[8]

We hope additional work will be done on how these teachings circulated globally and also the impact they have had on third-culture missionary families.

The Cycle Repeats

As we were writing this book, major news outlets were taking notice of tradwife influencers. While today's tradwife aesthetic carries unique cultural touchpoints, we see clear parallels with older evangelical resources. Dominionist and Quiverfull ministries like Above Rubies and Vision Forum are trad-culture prototypes, and many of the ideals overlap. We also see modern-day self-platformed influencers on X (formerly Twitter) and

YouTube talking about promised generational legacies and how birthing children can help make America a Christian nation, sentiments that echo resources that were popular during the '90s and '00s. Because these teachings come with an aesthetic, it's easy to spot the rebrand in them, but recycled ideas are not limited to the Dominionist and Quiverfull corners of the Christian parenting library.

We also read contemporary secular resources like Abigail Shrier's *Bad Therapy* (2024) and recognized familiar arguments that decry "soft" parenting methods, present a laundry list of parental fears as motivators, and call for harsher parenting styles.[9] The "fears" of the moment may be different, but Shrier's recipe resembles the one Dobson used in *Dare to Discipline*.

It's important to note that these ideas keep getting recycled, even though their impacts are no longer theoretical. There are children who have grown up in homes shaped by them. Parents of now-adult children articulate what the promises offered by these resources and "experts" have wrought. Homeschooling alumni network online to identify the impact of culture-war motivated homeschooling. Substack and podcast communities collectively process what it was like to be raised by Dobson's principles. Women write memoirs spotlighting the harms of the Dominionist ideals.[10] Survivors of abuse enabled by family-life teaching tell their stories.[11] There is plenty of real, already-lived-out fruit at hand to examine, and some of it has to do with the moral failures of the leaders themselves.

Vision Forum's Doug Phillips, for instance, settled out of court after being credibly accused of sexually assaulting the family's live-in nanny, a stay-at-home daughter who moved in with them as a minor.[12] Larry Tomczak was embroiled in the Sovereign Grace Church abuse scandal and accused of "repeatedly assaulting a woman with plastic and wooden sticks" beginning "when she was a child and last[ing] more than two decades," including beating her bare bottom as an adult.[13]

Doug Wilson is accused of failing to report abuse, welcoming a known pedophile into the community, and arranging for him to marry a young woman of the community, after which the perpetrator reoffended—among other things.[14] Ten women sued Bill Gothard for sexual abuse, harassment, and rape, and the Institute in Basic Life Principles disaffiliated from him.[15] Gary Ezzo was excommunicated due to allegations of overbearing leadership from several churches, including Grace Community Church, a megachurch overseen by John MacArthur.[16] MacArthur himself has been credibly accused of excommunicating women for refusing to reconcile with abusive husbands (one now jailed for sexually assaulting his children).[17] We believe the connection isn't coincidental. Evangelical churches have been "focused on the family" for decades, which means problems found in evangelical family-life teaching mirror what is occurring in evangelical church family systems.

The Church as Dysfunctional Family

The New Testament relies on the family as a metaphor for the church. Paul employs imagery of a nursing mother and exhorting father. Christians refer to themselves as brothers and sisters. Church leaders are spiritual fathers and mothers in the faith. These powerful words aren't just rhetorical features. They also name the reality that, like those familial roles, the church has tremendous power to hurt or heal.

As we read many of these parenting resources, we quickly came to identify how the authorial *tone* often matched the teaching. Tedd Tripp writes with an earnest zeal that one can almost feel through the page when he claims, "Only God can slake the thirst of [a child's] soul for relationship."[18] Nancy Campbell uses nurturing language to respond to "the constant cry . . . from young women. . . . 'Oh that I had an older mother to lead me and show me the right way.' This is a heart cry across the nations."[19] John Rosemond writes with assuredness, for parents and experts alike: "'Because I said so' is a statement of leadership. It affirms a parent's authority."[20] By contrast, Jim and Lynne Jackson decided to "lure parents in with inspiration about building wisdom and encouragement." Jim and Lynne describe their work as the "pie fingers" found in cartoons, visual steam that attracts hungry parents to an enticing feast. This tone of encouraging empowerment is evident in the tone of their resources.[21]

In many ways, parents consuming these materials are being, well, *parented* by the pastor-teachers. So, too, congregants are being parented by spiritual leaders. The way children in families are expected to behave parallels the ways church members are expected to behave. Pastor-teachers who focus on hierarchy and compliance often have extensive procedures for church discipline and expectations regarding their own pastoral authority that extend deeply into a member's life. Churches where children are expected to comply without question may discover that pastors cannot be questioned either.

These dynamics reinforce one another, and while we'd be hard-pressed to identify which is cause and which is effect, we can say that Christian family-life teaching doesn't just impact individual families. It reverberates through entire churches, even denominations, and—in turn—shapes the culture of different corners of the church. The parallels are also obvious in the ways "children" in the system are treated when they attempt to individuate or identify problems. Do the "parents" have the capacity to listen? Will people be shamed for challenging leaders and asking questions, or will they be pressured to comply, and—if they don't—experience a painful spiritual orphaning?

This is important to keep in mind, because the things listed in the next section apply to immediate, extended, and also church "families."

Correlation with Abuse

Many of the recommendations of the books and resources we evaluated were applied behind closed doors and according to the subjective discernment of parents who believed themselves to be acting in God's stead or according to divine endorsement. This enabled abuse, especially in communities where other families operated by the same methods.

> There was no accountability for [my mother's] actions, even when our church found out how far things had gone. We were regularly left with marks on our bodies. Usually, they were in hidden places under clothes. The ultra conservative modesty rules helped keep her tracks hidden. The few times that marks were more visible on spots like our arms or faces, other parents in the community explained it away. My mother would joke with others, "I had to spank her five times in the past hour!" And other moms would just laugh.
>
> —Autumn

People raised in Christian Fellowship Center churches of upstate New York describe community gatherings where any adult could spank any child for any reason.[22] Toby Sumpter, a pastor at Doug Wilson's influential Christ Church, tweeted about how the church has "discipline rooms" for parents, so they can spank children mid-service,[23] and Larry Tomczak describes a similar practice in the Sovereign Grace churches.[24] Some parents told us how they were ostracized or excommunicated for *not* spanking their children, and many adults described their concerns for children within their communities who they knew were regularly spanked. These individuals didn't know *how* to advocate for children without further isolating them and alienating their parents or risking escalating the abuse. When a community endorses or directly teaches spanking, it is much harder for parents to choose other means.

Corporal punishment doesn't hurt children only in the moment; it also grooms them for further abuse.

The spanking manuals include instructions such as the following: Take a child somewhere private, give them spiritual instruction, pull down their pants, spank their bare bottom, and offer hugs and prayers afterward. This recipe communicates to children that it's okay for adults to hurt their bodies in private places, because God says so. It also requires children to "be reconciled" afterward. When this is practiced over and over—and when additional spankings come if they protest!—children are taught to expect this treatment. This leaves them vulnerable to anyone who might say, "God wants me to do this; I'm doing this because I love you; even though I hurt your body, you must show me affection and act reconciled." This is even more the case when this messaging comes from a spiritual authority figure or someone at the top of a hierarchy who demands unquestioning obedience. Liturgized spanking *trains* children and grooms them for sexual and other kinds of abuse in direct ways, and the same problematic messaging occurs with other retributive punishment methods rooted in the idea that God requires parents to inflict pain and shame.

When children learn that love is painful or that it's okay for someone to hurt them or speak authoritatively about their internal motives, they are susceptible to intimate partner violence in the future.[25] Not only does abuse feel "normal," but when it's entwined with other Christian teachings about submission or laying down one's life to serve others, it follows that people raised with these practices may be ill-equipped to identify poor treatment and to seek help or leave a relationship. In fact, they may crave a kind of painful way of relating because that feels like "love." We heard from adults who found themselves needing to ask an intimate partner to hurt their body in order for them to feel forgiven and okay again. And others found ways to punish or deny themselves if they failed to act perfectly.

Multiple respondents traced the beginning of self-harm practices such as cutting to childhood lessons in which affection and forgiveness came only after physical punishment. We also heard from children who experienced unwanted and confusing sexual arousal during spanking sessions. This is biologically understandable and underscores the way spanking can overlap with sexual abuse. Children who experienced this found it impacted their sexual function and desires into adulthood.[26]

> Spanking completely overwhelmed my nervous system, and along with the fear and pain there came arousal. Especially the times I was spanked on a bare bottom, it was a horrible mixture of shame, pain, fear, and sexual arousal. I had no idea as a young child that was happening for me. I was just very confused by my response to it.
>
> —Matt

Additionally, sometimes the very manuals themselves became a source of confusion and pain to children. Some people recalled acting out scripted "spanking" games with siblings or noted how reading the liturgies of spanking found in these books became associated with sexual arousal.

> An odd and embarrassing thing for me with those parenting books in those early adolescent years is that I experienced spanking as unintentional sexual abuse/sexual assault. . . . I had a habit of . . . reading those Christian parenting books that were advocating spanking and going into detail about how it should be done.
>
> —MC

Christian teachers and parents: Please don't shut your ears to the adults naming the abuses they endured as children. This is an impossible and heartbreaking reckoning, and no human calculators can provide an accurate ledger. We know that Jesus cares about every child who adults mistreated (see Matt. 18:6). Many of the methods described in parenting books also include heavy-handed teaching alongside punishment and the relentless delivery of Scripture, instruction, and correction, which later destroyed people's faith. More and more people are *explicitly naming family of origin dynamics as an impetus* for their rejection of faith or disaffiliation with the church, and this should sober every single Christian.

Many parents were themselves operating under heavy-handed preaching and teaching that offered constant threats of fearful outcomes and coercion into very specific theological frameworks. In a sense, parents were sometimes victims of high-control religion while also becoming victimizers. Sometimes teaching relied on "spiritual bypassing," or using theological or biblical prescriptions to cope with sorrow and difficulty. When children are told to choose a "happy heart" regardless of their feelings, any undesirable emotion is reframed with Bible verse catechesis and "choosing joy." Mind versus emotion quickly becomes mind *over* emotion. Spiritual bypassing can also happen at the parental level (where parents are told to mistrust their intuition or "put off" their God-given emotions that may be raising red flags) or at a community level (where the bluster of the group covers the secret pain of what's really happening in individual hearts and families).

Expectations for instant obedience also normalize codependency and a denial of personhood in children raised in these homes. Because a child's autonomy is denied from very early on, and they are told to constantly and cheerfully comply with authority figures, children learn not to ask questions. They learn to bend to the demands of anyone they perceive to be an authority figure or, in the case of girls catechized into the gender hierarchies we discussed in chapter 3, any male at all. They learn to look to someone else to teach them the "right way" to live.

Training children into unquestioning compliance deprives them of opportunities to practice agency and to make decisions. Rather than gaining experience in how to make wise choices, how to consider their own desires and interests, how to make mistakes and recover from them, children are taught to constantly—even scrupulously—obey. This hijacks critical thinking and leaves adults poorly equipped to understand their own desires and motivations. It creates an attachment to authority figures who will diagnose people's hearts for them. This can give rise to a kind of spiritual codependency, in which people then seek out their own version of omnicompetent voices—religious or not—to tell them how to live the "right way" or are paralyzed by indecision.

In these ways, American evangelical family-life teaching cultivated narcissistic parenting. When children are viewed as extensions of godlike parents, individuation and differentiation—developmental stages in which young adults separate in distinct ways from their family of origin and establish their own sense of self—may be delayed well into adulthood. Christian teaching that children are "arrows" or "godly seed" for future generations exacerbated this, raising the stakes for compliance and strengthening parental expectations. This tracks with many stories we heard from adult children who were compliant all through their teenage years, and it wasn't until their thirties or forties that they began to "rebel" against their parents. Sometimes this was sparked by their becoming parents themselves, which put their own parents' methods and motivations in a new light. Sometimes adult children realized that inauthentic connection or betraying their own values and beliefs was the price of a relationship with their parents. If they began dating someone or chose a career a parent disapproved of, or if they had doubts about Christianity, or even if they switched denominations or started voting differently, they found themselves rejected by their parents. In these cases, the cost of an adult child's personhood and autonomy was a painful estrangement from extended family members.

For the parents' part, they found themselves confused by this outcome. Because requiring compliance had "worked" when children were young and, to an extent, even through adolescence, when adult children eventually exercised autonomy, parents found it hard to tolerate any perspective but their own. Why were the godly children they had so carefully trained, who they had been proud to see following the right path, suddenly apostatizing? Diligent parents were dismayed to discover "the theft of values [they'd] worked so hard to instill."[27] Parents of "prodigals" also experienced isolation and shame.

Again, we are not here to judge *intent*. We imagine many of these parents would say they did the best they could, they loved their children more than anything, and they still want God's best for them, but the framework they had been offered told them that parents who love their children *control* them and can expect that good Christian parenting will set children on a permanent, parent-approved course. And children had been taught that loving their parents equaled *complying* without question. This combination is unsustainable for adult human relationships, and changing the pattern requires both parties to actively work at it. We did hear from parents who listened and attempted new ways of relating; we also heard from adult children who recognized their parents' efforts in this area. We heard from others, though, who were stuck in hampered relationships, primarily because parents were still invested in being right.

Many of the popular Christian parenting resources were written by young parents. James Dobson wrote *Dare to Discipline* when he had a preschooler and infant at home. Ginger Hubbard had elementary-age children. Larry Tomczak had a toddler. Gothard had no children at all. We've already noted how many experts lacked credentials or relevant expertise, but the insight they brought to their work was without question immature, underdeveloped, and short-sighted as well. Even people like Tedd Tripp or Abbie Halberstadt, who wrote their books with teenagers in the home, did not have the experience and perspective of parenting adult children, let alone the time and space to consider the fruit.

Reb Bradley reflected on his adult daughter's parenting: "I just wish that what my daughter is doing with her kids," he told us during an interview, "I wish I had understood that when she and her brothers and sisters were younger."[28] Bradley claims he attempted to revise his earlier work after he realized this, but the vast majority of these resources remain unchanged from their original printing or have been only slightly updated.

In fact, it was startling to read Roy Lessin's book and Bruce Ray's book right after reading Ginger Hubbard's book *Don't Make Me Count to Three*, one of the top titles still recommended to Christian mothers on Instagram. Reading these books in swift succession, it became clear that Hubbard had pulled major sections and structural outlines almost verbatim from Lessin's and Ray's works.[29] Hubbard thanks Lessin in her acknowledgments and is forthright about basing her work on Tripp's, but concerns about plagiarism aside, the recycling of unexamined ideas leads to the perpetuation of methods that probably would be rejected under different circumstances. We don't know if moms in 2024 would intentionally recommend Lessin's 1979 book *Spanking: Why? When? How?* or Ray's *Withhold Not Correction* (1978), but that is essentially what they are doing when they circulate Hubbard's 2003 book. These experts elude transparency and accountability, yet today's parents are left, like the generations before them, to place their trust in recycled claims, implement their ideas, and wait for the receipt to come due.

And it will. We originally titled this book *Lies Christian Parents Believe* because so many of the talking points found in Christian parenting books are not particularly Christian—by which we mean *identifiable with the life and teaching of Jesus.* Despite the heavy emphasis on consequences for a child's misbehavior, one of the biggest lies Christian parents believe is that their own actions do not have consequences. They expect to be judged by their intentions and not their actions. But the reality is that parents aren't kings and queens. Children don't *belong* to parents in the sense of ownership. Parents cannot control the choices of future generations. Parents are not godlike agents of authority. Parents are simply human beings, people entrusted with the care of vulnerable children for a short time.

Many times during the course of writing this book, I (Marissa) thought about Jesus's parable of the unmerciful servant. In it, a servant owes his master a great deal, an impossible-to-pay amount. Facing prison and punishment, he panics, only to discover that his master is merciful and discharges the debt, sending him on his way. But shortly thereafter the servant finds a person under his own authority, someone who owes much less, and demands an accounting—cruelly exacting retribution without mercy.

This story speaks to something true about the human condition, about the way we eagerly receive and welcome mercy for ourselves while placing expectations for perfection onto the shoulders of others. Christian parents do this in many ways:

when they sing and talk and write about the goodness of God's grace and forgiveness, but then they turn around and tell their children, "God wants me to spank you";

when they advocate for parental rights for themselves but dismiss or are threatened by conversations about children's rights;

when they probe their children's hearts for sin while never asking whether their own judgments and motivations might be impaired by sin;

when they speak and preach and teach from the pulpit with omnicompetent certainty but when things go bad can only offer, "But that's not what we intended";
when the fruit of their teaching is rotten.

This is a painful and humbling reckoning for those courageous enough to make it, but I believe there is no way forward without telling the truth.

We suspect pastors and helping professionals know that the receipt is coming due already, because they are working with adult children and parents who are navigating these difficult dynamics, often in secrecy and shame. We also suspect that this book comes on the very front end of a long overdue conversation, with some families looking for ways to heal while a new generation of parents looks for alternate ways forward. This leaves everyone asking, "So where do we go from here?"

9

MOVING BEYOND THE MYTHOLOGY

> Train up a child in the way he should go:
> and when he is old, he will not depart from it.
>
> —Proverbs 22:6 KJV

We started this book by noting that this verse from Proverbs is often presented as a promise. *If* parents do parenting right, *then* their children will turn out the right way. Parenting is daunting, and mythical promises like these offer comfort in the absence of certainty. However, Proverbs and the genre of wisdom literature as a whole aren't meant to be read as guarantees or single-verse takeaways. Proverbs contains poetic imagery, parallelism, and a richly layered, intentional structure intended to cultivate wisdom and the fear of the Lord. Old Testament scholar Bruce Waltke translates this verse as follows: "Dedicate the youth according to his way. Even when he grows old he will not depart from it."[1] Note the phrase *should go* is not in Waltke's translation. Why? *Because that phrase isn't in the original Hebrew.*

The good-Christian-parenting empire runs on the assumption that parental intentionality will achieve certain results. There's a lot of hope hanging on the interpretive "in the way he should go" reading of this proverb. But what if the proverb is talking about something less prescriptive, something more broad? How does the meaning change if we understand "train up" to mean "dedicate," as Waltke translates the primary verb? This word is also used in reference to dedicating temples or consecrating holy things.[2] It carries a sense of setting something apart for religious use, but dedicators are typically not in power over houses or temples being consecrated. More specifically, parents committing their children to God's ways are doing so from a posture of walking alongside them rather than maintaining control over them. They may *dedicate*, but they cannot *determine*.

Waltke's translation also highlights the personhood of the young man in question: "the youth" (as opposed to "a youth") and "his way" (as opposed to a specific way or even a parent's preferred way). This phrasing spotlights the agency of *the known-and-knit-together-by-God child*.[3] Instead of Proverbs 22:6 being a promise of hoped-for results, the proverb observes that young adults are influenced by their childhood formation *and are also* active agents in their own lives. This perspective aligns with the overall authorial purpose of the book of Proverbs, which is to instruct young men to cultivate discernment so that they might choose for themselves between wisdom and folly.

We suggest that this proverb is not *prescriptive* but rather *descriptive*. Lessons learned in childhood, particularly ones that carry spiritual meaning, have lifelong impact. In that sense, entire Christian families were indeed "trained up" in various ways—parents bought into mythical parenting methods, children were raised in those ways, and generations were shaped by them. But where have those ways led them? And is there an off-ramp for those who want to find an alternate path forward?

For Adults Reflecting Back

We recognize that not everyone reading this book is a parent or is actively parenting. We also imagine many readers are seeking insight into their own past experiences as children or parents. If this is you, you may well be asking, "Where do *I* go from here?" We know our book won't speak to everyone's experience, but we hope that you have found touchpoints for your own story and vocabulary to name where you've been.

As we examined Christian parenting resources, we thought of what it must have been like for children to live under these teachings, and it broke our hearts. When we began to interview people, the imagined reality took on personal shape. Sometimes we saw faces online or heard stories of very early years still carried in the hearts and minds of adults. We recognize that these are tender places, and it was an immense honor and privilege to bear witness to some of your experiences. In many cases, we heard about deep pain and unbearable sorrow.

If you resonate with that, we are so sorry. We wish your parents and the parenting experts who inspired them had offered a better way. We wish that other adults in your life could have protected you. Often, people's stories of what happened in their homes were tangled up with what went on in their churches or homeschooling groups or other faith gatherings, and we wish that your communities had safeguarded you.

We are writing in a moment when conversations about trauma and abuse have been subsumed by the culture wars, including in the church. There are enclaves of the church that dismiss people's suffering, blaming them for wallowing in victimhood. When we hear such sentiments, we hear echoes of popular Christian parenting teaching: Stop crying; choose joy; God will not give you more than you can handle; be reconciled with the parent who spanked you; whining is a sin; and on and on. We reject these talking points that dismiss the reality of trauma, domestic abuse, and the ways those closest and most dear can cause deep and lasting pain. Instead, we want to own and name the truth: Christian teaching from Christian pastor-teachers in Christian communities has hurt people in unspeakable and inexcusable ways. It's understandable to want to believe that harmful teaching is "not really Christian." But the parental guidance we have examined was marketed as "biblical" and "Christian" to thousands of families, and parents and children believed it to be such. That matters.

We hope that our work here has shown that doctrinal and theological preferences have real-life impact; they are never theoretical. We also hope that our work has identified areas where this teaching and advice that was sold to people is deeply destructive. There is a pressing need to examine our ideas about parenting in light of the life and teaching of Jesus.

If you find yourself on the front end of exploring your family of origin dynamics or suspect that what happened to you was not okay, we hope it helps to get this affirmation: If families followed the teachings in many of these resources (and we have heard from many parents and adult children alike who testify to this), people were abused in the name of God.

We also recognize that *how* teachings played out for individuals and families is as unique and varied as each individual family. This is, in some ways, evidence that a one-size-fits-all approach to parenting simply doesn't work. Some parents adopted practices only piecemeal or made choices that mitigated the harm of various teachings. Some families followed elements of popular recommendations and did not experience problematic outcomes. Sometimes extended families or healthy faith communities buffered people from the full impact. Other times, the family unit may have been operating in healthy ways with parents unaware of what their children were learning in different subcultures. We were also glad to hear from people who did not experience significant negative impact from the Christian parenting resources we cover in this book. If this is you, we think your experience matters too. We are thankful for that outcome and hope that you still found value and resonance in our work. In case it needs saying, your story matters too.

We also recognize that many Christian communities feature strong messaging about reconciliation, grace, honoring one's parents, and forgiveness. This is understandable. We are people who have received mercy; freely we have received, and freely we want to give. However, we believe that forgiveness doesn't mean offering dangerous people access into one's life, or that love equals pain, or that one's dignity and autonomy should be sacrificed catering to the needs and desires of others. Many children who were raised in homes that practiced these harmful teachings learned early on to subsidize the cost of family harmony by ignoring their own needs, always saying yes, and never learning how to defend themselves or even offer a different point of view. We suspect that if you resonate with this, you may have other clues in your life that these approaches aren't working well for you. Enmeshed family relationships may hamper mental, spiritual, or physical health and well-being; may require you to sacrifice other relationships; or may contribute to addictions, unhealthy coping mechanisms, or other negative behavioral choices. Perhaps a change in your life—beginning a new relationship, welcoming a new child, moving to a new community, or starting a new job—has prompted you to reconsider things.

How you choose to navigate your relationships is up to you, because you *do* have agency and autonomy. Should you choose to seek support from therapists or pastors or spiritual directors, we suggest you look for qualified people who have some awareness of religious trauma. For pastors and other professionals who may be coming alongside people navigating these complicated dynamics, we hope you will consider the messaging that children raised in these families have been receiving since birth and how as a result they may need unique pastoral care and counsel.

When we write or speak about these things, we also hear from parents who carry deep regrets. Some express overwhelming shame and heartbreak. Some of these parents feel in retrospect that because they put too much trust in the promises of parenting experts, they ended up hurting or abusing their children. This can be a devastating realization, and if this is you, we are so sorry. When we say that this teaching betrayed entire families, we have this painful reality in mind.

Whether you are taking the first steps toward listening or are already far down the path of truth-telling, we want to say to you *well done*. Being willing to lay down defensiveness and listen to the ways your actions hurt your loved ones—whatever your intentions may have been—is significant.

There's also work to be done. Naming dynamics is the first step toward attempting repair. We can't promise you that doing this work will lead to connection with your adult children. We can't tell you what attempting repair looks like in your specific situation. But we think it's likely that not doing anything or remaining defensive or fragile will continue to impair closeness and connection with your children.

We suggest that now is a moment to get curious about your own framework, to ask yourself what drew you to that kind of teaching in the first place, what made it feel *right* to you at the time, or, if it didn't, what led you to ignore your intuition. A licensed mental health professional with experience in family systems, high-control religion, or religious trauma may be especially supportive as you work through this. Cultivating the skills to practice intentional, empathetic listening may also be a help. Many of the approaches in these books leave parents particularly ill-equipped to listen to and accept the alternate viewpoints of their children, whatever their age. Practicing how to listen, how to reflect back what you are hearing, and how to grow your tolerance for differences will likely be worthwhile.

We also encourage you to read through the next section. Though it's written with people actively parenting in mind, we think you will find helpful ideas that apply to you as well.

For Parents Moving Forward

We regularly hear from parents who say something along the lines of "I appreciate these critiques, but what is a resource that you *do* recommend?" This question is understandable. As parents ourselves, we relate to the desire to have trustworthy alternatives and guidance in charting a healthier path forward.

As we read dozens of resources, we took note of the ease with which well-intentioned people position themselves to speak authoritatively on parenting topics, often without relevant expertise or education, or position their own experiences as parents as normative for everyone else. While we, as individuals, do have various resources or approaches we might personally recommend, we recognize that our own unique family dynamics, histories, and cultures, as well as the temperaments and needs of our individual children, all play into those recommendations. We might be willing to share resource suggestions with friends we know personally, but using the platform of this book to do so enables the very system we are critiquing.

Instead, we invite parents to reclaim their agency and autonomy. We'd like to *equip you* to cultivate a wisdom that enables you to grow in your understanding of your family background and history, the unique needs and personalities of the children entrusted to you, and the strengths and weaknesses of different methodologies. Here are some general areas to get curious about.

Getting Curious About Responses

Jim and Lynne Jackson of Connected Families encourage parents to pause and reflect on what they are thinking and feeling at any given moment. They explain how "taking a deep breath and double-checking messages" can help parents understand their own upbringing in order to make wise choices in the present.[4] Parenting is an all-encompassing task that can have parents operating through in-the-moment responses without the chance to reflect. It can be difficult to carve out space to ask, "How am *I* coming into the room as a mother or a father? What do I bring with me when I arrive at this vocation of parenting?" The Jacksons include this as a first step for all parents to pause and reflect in a four-step framework: Foundation (You are safe with me), Connect (You are loved no matter what), Coach (You are called and capable), Correct (You are responsible for your actions).[5] So in a similar vein, it may be a help for parents to ask, "What is going on with *me*?"

This is difficult but important work, and different seasons of parenting can be an invitation to revisit childhood or extend to today's children things previous generations of adults were unable to offer. Christian parents might see in this an opportunity to apply the "one anothering" verses to parenting—forbearing with the weak; restoring those who sin gently; being compassionate, humble, and tenderhearted; and practicing the fruit of the Spirit. Approaching children with love, joy, peace, forbearance, kindness, goodness, faithfulness, gentleness, and self-control is evidence of the Holy Spirit working in a believer's life. Also, as adults cultivate empathy and compassion, letting go of the high standards that keep people stuck in perfectionism or fear, they might discover curiosity and tenderness for parents or other caregivers who were unable to offer the kindness they longed for.

Getting Curious About Families of Origin

Family of origin dynamics shape the way people approach parenting. This can manifest as vows to never repeat certain patterns from their own childhood experiences or an attempt to replicate things they did appreciate. But there can also be specific instances in everyday parenting interactions that unexpectedly trigger emotions or leave parents operating instinctively according to unexamined principles absorbed in childhood. For example, if adults were raised as children to obey right away without question, it can feel intolerable, dangerous even, when their children don't respond that way. If adults were raised in environments where children were expected to behave perfectly, it can be difficult to admit one's parenting mistakes. Parenting will almost certainly bring up things from a parent's own childhood, and without some attention to this, adults can reenact their own childhood responses or end up stuck in unintentional patterns.

A mom reached out one day on Instagram. She described how scared she was because she couldn't stop yelling at and spanking her children, no matter how hard she tried. She connected this pattern back to her own childhood, when she had been frequently spanked. When her children misbehaved, she was reactive and violent, and then she would feel guilty and pray and try to stop. But everything would repeat. This exemplifies how deeply rooted parenting responses can be, and it may take long-term, strategic effort to do the difficult work of recognizing what's going on in *you* while simultaneously finding new tools and approaches to relate to *children*.

We appreciate this parent's courage and willingness to name her behavior and to acknowledge that it wasn't okay and that it was hurting her children. Prayer is good, but parents in situations like this need *help*, and children need *advocates*. Children cannot advocate for themselves, so that means adults must speak out on their behalf. This may mean braving the discomfort of questioning other parents when we hear them joke about spankings or "losing it" with their children or challenging distorted parenting teaching coming from the pulpit or bookstore. It may mean that we involve a trusted therapist, a pastor, or other authorities so we can actionably help safeguard children. We want to strongly encourage Christian adults to stop prioritizing the comfort of adults over the well-being of children. However, this need not be a zero-sum choice. We can advocate for the well-being of children while also seeking to help parents heal and giving them access to sound resources.

A licensed mental health counselor, a spiritual director, or a trusted personal friend can help parents gain insight into ways their family of origin, lifestyle stressors, personality, or other factors can be keeping them stuck. We suggest critically examining the credentials and bias of anyone you invite to speak into your life in this way. We've written about some of the shortcomings of biblical counseling and the unwillingness to consider external sources of authority. There are biblical counselors out there who are open to insight from the fields of mental health and social sciences; even still, we encourage you to ask careful questions of any counselors. Similarly, there is no standardized credentialing of pastors or church staff members, so it is beneficial to query whether a pastoral counselor has the experience and training necessary to help you. Asking a pastor if and when they would refer you to someone else with additional expertise can be a way to see if they are willing to recognize their own limitations and defer authority to professionals outside the church.

If there have been different topical chapters in this book that have resonated with you, we suggest exploring those themes with a qualified therapist or spiritual director:

- How were manhood, womanhood, boyhood, and girlhood viewed in your family, and how has that impacted you?
- What was communicated regarding obedience and disobedience in your family growing up?
- Did you feel seen and respected as a human being?
- What did you learn about sin and atonement as a child?
- Were you spanked as a child? How did that impact you?

These questions might be helpful springboards to explore ways your personal experiences intersect with Christian parenting mythology and, in turn, your parenting. If you are co-parenting with a partner or spouse, discussing these topics can help bring relational awareness to this partnership as well.

Getting Curious About Children

We've written about the way popular resources dehumanize children or view them as extensions of their parents. The antidote to this is viewing a child as an individual created by God with a God-given right to autonomy as they grow into adulthood and make their own choices. Children bear the image of God, something that is not based on what they do or how they perform or their connection to parents: It is who they are. Children are also some of every Christian's nearest and newest neighbors. As C. S. Lewis wrote in his essay "The Weight of Glory," "There are no ordinary people. You have never talked to a mere mortal. . . . Next to the Blessed Sacrament itself, your neighbor is the holiest object presented to your senses."[6]

Reframing an anthropology of children around the awe-inspiring, miraculous nature of children as human beings can help parents let go of latent beliefs that children are theirs to mold or adversaries to conquer. Besides, from a Christian perspective, all children are *God's* children—they belong to him. It can be sobering as a parent to realize that we are stewarding the charge of another human being. It's also freeing, because the outcome doesn't depend on parental efforts. Christian parents can entrust children and their future to God. This perspective shift can, we hope, put an end to seeing children as empty buckets to fill or arrows for parents to shoot or testimonies for the witness of the church or any other aspirational desire. Instead, parents can appreciate the miracle of the child who stands before them in real time, taking their temperaments and developmental needs into account.

Learning from people who have devoted their lives and whole areas of research to observing children's behavior, brains, and bodies can help parents identify ways children grow and develop. Adults can also ask children what life is like for them. Most of us live in an adult-oriented world, so it will take effort to cultivate empathy for a child's perspective: What is this expectation like for them? How does this consequence or punishment land with them? Sometimes simply *listening* to a child in a neutral moment can uncover helpful information: Perhaps they aren't dawdling to be rebellious; perhaps they have difficulty focusing on the task or are worried about making a mistake. This will also "train *you* up" to connect with and respectfully listen to children, something we think will serve parents well in the long term.

Learning what behaviors are age appropriate, learning how to interpret behavior as communication, learning what children are capable of, learning how they receive information and digest it, and learning about things like neurodivergence and disability can help parents interact in healthy ways and think critically about their expectations and the advice they are getting from various resources. Engaging with children as human beings means that dehumanizing rhetoric will quickly strike a discordant note.

In Christian cultures that have high expectations for performance, good behavior, and Christian excellence, reevaluating frameworks—including the high expectations we have for ourselves—can require intentional and persistent work. The ever-elusive quest for a "right way" speaks to the constant spiritual treadmill to which most evangelicals have become accustomed. It can be unmooring to set aside the checklists and charts that reassure us we're doing it right. It can be humbling to recognize we've made mistakes and to attempt repair, especially if we've always been held to standards of perfection. It can feel like free-falling to rely on long-buried intuition or brand-new skills, but the discomfort can be an invitation to continue pressing into personal growth as well.

Getting Curious About Experts

We've talked at length about how prosperity gospel parenting formulas and myths are appealing because they offer the reassurance that parents are doing things right. That is comforting and helps shuffle some of the responsibility for this often-overwhelming task onto the shoulders of others. But reclaiming trust in parental intuition doesn't mean that parents have nothing to learn or that their opinions and instincts are authoritative and unquestionable. We suggest a posture of confident humility: confidence in one's own capacity, God-given instincts, and grace for a family's needs in every respect alongside a true humility that knows personal shortcomings, regularly confesses sins, and is willing to receive guidance.

This will equip parents to critically examine resources and check motivations. A parent who's examined their own past and recognized, for example, that they were taught to cheerfully obey, will be able to identify that they may be drawn to parenting resources that are written from an authoritative, unquestioning point of view. A parent who's able to identify that their childhood was chaotic may be able to observe when they are drifting toward techniques and methodologies that promise guaranteed outcomes.

Here are some questions we think might help you as you consider which resources to trust:

- How did I come across this resource? Was it recommended to me? By whom? A friend, an algorithm, a pastor, or a slick marketing campaign?
- Why do I trust the person offering advice? Do I know them personally? Am I able to see real-time fruit of their teaching? Or are they a name on a printed book or a face behind a screen or a curated Instagram feed?
- What are their credentials? Do they bring a particular angle of education or expertise? If they are parents, how old are their children? Are the claims they are making in line with the reality of their experience?
- Does this expert acknowledge their own limitations? Do they encourage me to learn from others or to come exclusively to them?

These questions are especially important in this age of social media and influencer culture, both of which are designed to build social connection through a curated lens. Social media can be a smoke-and-mirrors way to build credibility, even more so than the print, radio, and ministry empires of yesteryear. In the best-case scenario, caring Christian communicators find themselves filling gaps beyond their skill set in the name of Christian ministry. It's a familiar path: Someone who wants to help other parents writes a book. It is successful, and they begin to encounter new opportunities. Perhaps they sense a call based on their success; isn't God opening doors? And they continue building what becomes a parenting empire. We're not here to try to evaluate someone's spiritual call, but a big platform doesn't necessarily equal a trustworthy ministry.

One way to counteract the pitfalls of relying on expertise is to listen to varied voices, intentionally choosing those that offer differing perspectives and cultural starting places. This not only staves off echo chambers but also keeps parents from believing they found the "one right way to parent." As a bonus, parents can fill their toolboxes with multiple approaches and may be more comfortable switching to a different method if something seems ill-suited to a specific child or season. In this way, sifting through the advice of experts can empower parents rather than place them under a heavy yoke. The appendix at the end of this book, "Tool for Evaluating Resources," includes a metric that we hope will be helpful for you as you evaluate resources and identify gaps that you'd like to shore up in different ways.

Getting Curious About Jesus

We recommend getting curious about Jesus. This may seem like an overly simplistic Sunday school suggestion, but after reviewing over a hundred Christian parenting resources that barely mention the name of Jesus, we think it needs saying. It's easy to slip the label of "Christian" onto any number of things—denominational affiliations, doctrinal frameworks, well-behaved families, moralism. But in its most basic sense, what makes something Christian is whether it reflects the life and teaching of Jesus.

This means Christian parents should prioritize becoming well-versed in the life and teaching of Jesus. Spend time in the Gospels. Read them regularly. Consider what Jesus is like, how he interacted with people, particularly children. The surest antidote to false claims made in his name is an educated understanding of how he lived and what he taught. Sometimes this can be a painful or difficult endeavor, particularly if you were raised in Christian communities.

> It just sucks to be told that "just knowing and listening" to Jesus or the gospel protects you, when it didn't. . . . It doesn't quite do

> justice to the soul-crushing difficulty of recognizing Jesus's voice when everything you used to think was his voice deeply harmed you. It's not that we don't want to listen; it's that we've lost any illusion that thinking we are hearing and understanding his voice, whether through Scripture or otherwise, is a guarantee that we actually are. We've been wrong when we most sincerely wanted to follow him.
>
> —Michelle

Keeping Our Eyes Open

Reckoning with the cost of destructive or careless teaching is painful, and our evaluation here doesn't change or undo any of the hurt endured; it won't restore broken relationships. It's humbling to write a book like this and come to the end, knowing that there is very little we can offer readers for healing, reassurance, or a clear path forward, but we want to close with an invitation.

Do you remember the children's fable "The Emperor's New Clothes"? In it, two men pretend to be tailors and sell the idea of an expensive and unique cloth that only the best kind of people can see. The vain and gullible king wants, indeed *must have*, the fabric. The "tailors" string the king along, measuring and waving thread through the air as if they are hemming and stitching. Neither the king nor his servants nor anyone in the royal court wants to reveal that *they* cannot see the fabric. The king eventually parades out to a gathering naked, believing himself adorned in a fabric that he and everyone else is only pretending to see. The illusion is broken when a child calls out something along the lines of "But, Mama, the king isn't wearing any clothes!"

Different storytellers conclude the story in different ways. In one version, the emperor is embarrassed and angry, but the swindling tailors flee before he can take them to task. In another version, the emperor knows the child speaks the truth, but he ignores it, refusing to acknowledge his error, and instead forges on—naked, ashamed, but determined to be right.

We are not trying to make a one-to-one comparison with this fable. We are not interested in judging the motivations of parenting experts, if such a thing were even possible, or in villainizing the "tailors." It's tempting to make the pastor-teachers the villains in this story—crooks who set out to swindle everyone or who operated with malice—but that would be an oversimplification. We expect that ministry motivations, lack of self-awareness, legitimate concerns and fears, marketing, greed, and the incapacity to reckon with consequences all play a part. We have attempted to present their teaching in their own words, and we hope that anyone who reads this book will not find their work unfairly represented, even if they find themselves disagreeing with us. Additionally, plenty of people looking for helpful advice found it in Christian parenting resources. To examine these resources critically is not to say there is nothing of merit in them or that all families were only harmed by them.

That being said, we think this fable offers a powerful picture of the current moment, when the American church is experiencing a widespread apocalyptic unveiling, when the evangelical empire is standing there, dressed up in the teaching and cultural garb of the past century. And those who were shaped by its influence are now asking, "But is there anything of *substance* there?" This is an important moment for the American church, and we invite Christians to approach the fable with that in mind. Will the *insiders*, the *Christians*, those who hold positions of leadership and influence, stiffen their necks and forge ahead—proud and naked, with all the hypocrisy and betrayal laid bare—and still insist on being *right*?

We hope not. Christians, whatever their intentions, are not infallible. Because we teach and preach—claiming to impart the Word of God—we need to reckon with the ways we get it wrong. Deconstruction is a necessary phase of spiritual development that every Christian undertakes at some point, perhaps multiple times. In 1 Corinthians 3, Paul addresses a situation in which Christians identified themselves as followers of specific teachers. He uses the metaphor of building to describe the work of these pastor-teachers (3:10–17), and he concludes that only what is constructed on the foundation of Christ Jesus will endure. Jesus holds up well to scrutiny. Indeed, many people who've exited church buildings find themselves still attached and even deeply committed to Jesus.

But Christian empires are built with all manner of materials. Some weigh people down with legalism and religious performativity. Paul warns that an exposing fire will lay all the work of Christian teachers bare, and perhaps this is what we are seeing as the fall of trusted leaders, hypocrisy, moral injury, and failed response to abuse disclosures empty the pews across denominations. Rather than being sobered by this thought, many Christian communities instead shame God's people, God's children, *God's building*, for questioning the quality of what they've been taught (1 Cor. 3:16–17). This is topsy-turvy, because, according to Paul, the revealing and refining is a necessary part of the work of cultivating discernment. While Paul's warning regarding fire is for the builders, the encouragement of verses 16–17 is *for all God's people*, reminding them of God's care and of the Holy Spirit in their midst.

Do Christians have the capacity to listen to the stories of the spiritual children of the church, to be angry and grieve and lament with those who sit among the ruins and to walk alongside those who want to rebuild? Is God incapable of preserving them—and all of us who make up the church (the sacred temple in whom he dwells!)—throughout this process? The pages of the psalms are filled with questions from lamenting children. God doesn't muffle or dismiss them. Indeed, the prophets remind people that performative, empty obedience is never the goal. Religious communities are repeatedly called to collective repentance, and the kings of Israel, tasked with religious faithfulness, are publicly chronicled according to the sins of their fathers. The idea that humans can build and enact faith communities impervious to critique is erroneous. It's okay to be honest about the church's failings.

We suggest that Christians not proceed from a posture of "How dare the children speak!" and "Shame on them for that tone!" Rather, let's be soberly aware that there's a day of reckoning for the emperors and tailors and pastors and parents and all who act as shepherds over God's people.

Ezekiel 34 poignantly describes shepherds, entrusted with the care of God's flock, who strengthen the weak, heal the sick, bind the injured, and bring back the strays. Doing this work requires communities to assume a collective responsibility and to prioritize the work of repair. It means a reordering of resources and attention, a casting down of the powerful and an exalting of the lowly, an unflinching attempt to humbly engage something that isn't crisply and mathematically defined—the unquantifiable damage of shipwrecked faith.

Because parenting teaching came with catechesis about what *God* is like, this is also a moment of iconoclasm, a moment to shatter the idols we've made out of parents, to tear down the high places where we've fashioned God after our own image. For those reading this book who still retain faith in God, we invite you to meet him afresh on his own terms.

Scripture depicts many families. None of them did things the "one right way." They all experienced dysfunction and heartbreak and, in many cases, what people today would consider trauma and abuse. One of the earliest stories involves Abraham and Sarah and Hagar. If you know it, you know it's a difficult one. At a certain point, Hagar and her son Ishmael are cast out of Abraham's extended family and abandoned to die. We invite you to imagine Hagar's story as a bridge between the adult children and the parents reading this book.

Hagar herself has been unfairly mistreated and rejected by family members who should've cared for her, and Hagar is also a mother who, weeping, abandons her son so she does not have to see him suffer. It's not a perfect parallel, but we suggest it powerfully depicts the generational devastation that can impact families. Christian families, too, experience loss and grief and anger and betrayal and things not being the way they were supposed to be. Hagar is the first character in the biblical narrative to name God herself. In that moment, she chooses the name The God Who Sees. And being seen by God does not come as a threat to ensure good behavior or with the fear of impending punishment but as a marker of his attention and love, a reminder that he cares. Foreshadowing the gospel, Hagar's name for God articulates that she has not been abandoned. Rather, in the midst of her difficulty and loss, God has witnessed her suffering and drawn near to save.

God, in fact, sees us up close. He saw Hagar. He saw Ishmael. He sees you. He always has. And when God decided to show us in human form what he is like, he didn't opt to come in the form of a king or queen, an earthly ruler high up in a hierarchy. God chose to come in the form of a baby, Immanuel, the God who is with us. The closing promise of Ezekiel 34, that the Lord himself will shepherd his flock, procuring safety and well-being for those once injured and scattered, is fulfilled in Jesus. And Jesus himself declares the work he came to do: to proclaim good news to the poor, freedom for the prisoners, recovery of sight for the blind; to set the oppressed free; and to proclaim the year of the Lord's favor (see Luke 4:14–21). This is the God who created every single one of us, who were all once children—prodigals and legalists alike. This is the God who rejoices over you, who sees everything you've endured, who knows your story, who is with you, and who loves you.

ACKNOWLEDGMENTS

From Kelsey

I am so incredibly blessed to have friends, family, and colleagues who have been cheerleaders, conversation partners, and tough-question-askers as this book took shape. Thank you to Keely Boeving for seeing the potential in this idea and for guiding and championing this book from the early stages of research and writing. Thank you to Katelyn Beaty and Stephanie Smith for advocating for this project and working with us to find the right balance of sharp analysis and sensitivity as we sought to deal with subject matter that is so fraught and tender for so many of our readers.

Thank you to the many people who have followed our work from the very beginning, from our first fumbling social media posts. When we started working on this project, we weren't sure who our audience would be, and we were amazed and grateful to find that there were so many thoughtful people with stories to tell, questions to ask, and ideas to share.

Thank you, Marissa, for responding to a random DM on Twitter and embarking on this journey with me. I have benefited so much from your wisdom and experience throughout this process, and I could not ask for a kinder or more generous coauthor.

Thank you, Mom and Dad, for being parents who let me ask big and uncomfortable questions. You introduced me to faith and helped me to remain curious. For that and much more, I am so grateful.

KC, my ever-patient husband and in-house editor, thank you for being an unfailing support. This book is better because I'm married to you. You ask hard questions, offer constructive criticism, and talk through my ideas—even the most half-baked ones.

Ida, Sam, and Helen, getting to know each of you as you grow is the greatest joy. This book is for you.

From Marissa

How grateful I am for the many people who helped make this book a reality! I count it a matchless gift to know each of you and am so thankful for your presence in my life.

Keely Boeving, I am so glad to have you as a literary agent! Thank you for your enthusiastic support for this project and for finding just the right home for this book.

Stephanie Smith, your early interest and investment in my and Kelsey's work helped shape our efforts, and Katelyn Beaty, your editorial insight and recommendations brought clarity and expert guidance. Thank you both for your editorial input.

Erin Smith, Jeremy Wells, Shelly MacNaughton, Julie Zahm, Kara Day, and all the others behind the scenes at Brazos and Baker who work hard to help turn documents into lovely books that wend their way into the hands of readers: many thanks.

To the individuals who responded to our survey and shared thoughts, observations, interviews, and snippets of your personal stories: Every time I return to these I am reminded of the courage required to share and sobered by the privilege of reading your words. Thank you for entrusting them to us.

To online friends Arlie, Jo, Sheila, Abbi, Heather, Jay, Matt, Rebekah, and so many others who've offered kind words: Your encouragement has been so nourishing. Thank you.

To patient friends who brainstormed and listened to me and heard more than I imagine they ever cared to about Christian parenting teaching, especially Katie, Casey, Christy, Renee, Jeremiah and Kristin, as well as the dear people who helped with babysitting, Meredith, Greta, Jessie, Elijah, and my parents: a thousand thanks.

Kelsey, I count our online connection and resulting working partnership and friendship to be one of the happiest Twitter surprises. What a grace it has been to work to bring this book to print alongside you. Thank you.

To my parents and brother: There is no hidden subtext in the writing of this book. I am grateful for each of you, for our family, and for everyone's continued commitment to healthy relationships. Mom and Dad, thank you for showing me what it looks like to prioritize family, to be willing to listen to adult children, and to never stop learning and growing. I love you.

TBBREG: You are all wonderful miracles, and I love that I get to know you and be in a family with you! I treasure the years of memories past and the thought of days ahead and take great delight in every moment I have with you. Thank you for your patience with me as I worked on this project, for your encouragement, and for your insights into family-life dynamics. I love you!

Aaron: What a remarkable and satisfying story it's been to write with our two lives. I so appreciate your support for my work and the way you care for all of us so well. I love you.

And to the Lord, the giver of all good things: Ever and always, thank you.

APPENDIX

TOOL FOR EVALUATING RESOURCES

As you evaluate a resource, indicate a *green*, *yellow*, or *red* rating for each question. At the end, tally up your totals for each color category. This will help you determine where to shelve the book.

Mostly Green: Top-shelf display cabinet. This is a resource to hold on to and return to.

Mostly Yellow Mixed with Some Green: Middle to low shelves. Give it some thought. Is it worth keeping? Why? Why not?

Mostly Yellow Mixed with Some Red: This is not the book for you. If you are an experienced parent and trust your intuition, jot down a few takeaways and don't keep the book.

Mostly Red: Straight into the trash.

QUESTIONS	GREEN LIGHT	YELLOW PAUSE	RED FLAG
Author Credentials	Author has credentials or experience relevant to the topic at hand.	Author has some credentials or experience, but they are not particularly relevant to parenting.	Author has no relevant credentials or experience.
Fruit	This resource came via recommendation from people I know and trust. I am able to see the fruit of this teaching in the lives of the author/teacher or people who apply it.	I have a general sense that this is a trusted resource. I like what I see of the community surrounding this author/teacher.	I have no way of evaluating the fruit of this teaching.
Biblical Blueprint	This resource acknowledges the uniqueness of every individual family.	This resource seems to present one perspective as normative for everyone.	This resource claims to speak with the voice of God.
Depiction of Children	This resource depicts children in respectful ways that acknowledge their humanity, including a consideration of child development, neurodivergence, and disability.	This resource is neutral or doesn't really mention children and their needs one way or the other.	This resource is dismissive of children, makes jokes at their expense, or demeans them.
Depiction of Parents	This resource depicts parents in respectful ways that acknowledge their humanity.	This resource is neutral or doesn't really mention parents and their needs one way or another.	This resource depicts parents in godlike ways or places impossible-to-meet expectations on them.
Depiction of Parent/Child Relationship	This resource depicts the parent-child relationship in honest and respectful ways.	This resource doesn't depict the parent/child relationship in a noticeable or mutual way.	This resource depicts the parent/child relationship in an antagonistic or one-sided way.
Discipline	This resource depicts discipline as instruction and offers varied ideas that any adult—including teachers, coaches, or pastors—could safely employ in public.	This resource seems to have one or two methods and little else. This resource is focused on behavior and compliance.	This resource offers suggestions that would be crimes if another adult employed them. This resource warns parents to discipline in secret.

QUESTIONS	GREEN LIGHT	YELLOW PAUSE	RED FLAG
Theology	This resource mentions Jesus and discusses his life and teaching. This resource acknowledges the rich diversity of the Christian faith.	This resource talks about Christian concepts but in either generic or very specific ways.	This resource bases parenting methods on heavy-handed doctrinal claims.
Language	This resource uses appropriate language.	This resource uses mostly appropriate language with some occasional problematic things.	This resource uses violent language or demeaning humor.
Tone	This resource is empowering, encouraging, and compassionate toward children and parents.	This resource is neutral in tone or is a mixture of empowerment and condemnation.	This resource is authoritarian in tone. It contains a lot of "shoulds" and "musts."
My Response	When I reflect on the suggestions in this resource, I am energized as a parent and appreciative of the time I have with my child.	This resource is neutral. There are some things that energized me and other things that discouraged me.	This resource lands like a heavy weight in my body. I feel like I need to buckle down and get to work—without complaining.
Takeaways	This resource enabled me to love my child better. I can identify many positive takeaways.	This resource provided some good ideas for me. I will probably apply some things and reject others.	This resource left me highly motivated to get parenting right. This resource left me feeling discouraged and like I've done everything wrong.
Totals			

NOTES

Preface

1. Over the past ten years, researchers and scholars have proposed newly nuanced or updated definitions of the term "evangelical." This research seeks to clarify the theological aspects and explore ways "evangelical" has become a religious, social, and political label. On the one hand, the term has become divisive and malleable; as we wrote this book, we wondered if we should avoid it altogether. On the other hand, historians, sociologists, theologians, and church leaders agree that this term is not meaningless. The term "evangelical" has been not only a way that a segment of American Protestants identify themselves but also a term scholars use to study American religion of the twentieth century; see, e.g., Robert Wuthnow, *Inventing American Religion: Polls, Surveys, and the Tenuous Quest for a Nation's Faith* (Oxford University Press, 2015).

We ultimately decided to rely on Daniel Vaca's understanding of American evangelicalism as a "commercial religion" that aims to reach the segment of American Protestants who purchase the books, music, and other forms of entertainment media labeled "Christian." Vaca writes, "Both the evangelical market and the evangelical population have taken shape continually, through commercial and cultural efforts. And if evangelicalism's growth has fueled industries that have supplied the demand of evangelicalism's consumers, the inverse has also occurred: industries have helped generate evangelical demand, evangelical identities, and the very idea of a coherent evangelical population." Daniel Vaca, *Evangelicals Incorporated: Books and the Business of Religion in America* (Harvard University Press, 2019), 2.

Vaca's framework is useful to us for a couple reasons. First, the literature we examine in this book is part of the phenomenon Vaca describes. Industry—in this case, the Christian parenting resource industry—has shaped and helped generate evangelical identity in the United States. Second, it questions consumer habits and in-group dynamics rather than precise theological commitments. In this book, we evaluate both the marketing techniques used to sell Christian parenting books and the reasons why Christian parents were convinced to purchase and trust them. As we will see, theological consistency is not the marker of the books we explore but rather they are united by a particular set of beliefs about religion in public life, the social and political functions of the family, and the moral state of the world.

Introduction

1. Justin Whitmel Earley, *Habits of the Household* (Zondervan, 2021), dedication page. This quotation is often attributed to Frederick Douglass, but there is no evidence in any of his published writings that this saying originated with him. See William Cheng, "The Radical Compassion of Frederick Douglass," Pacific Standard, February 14, 2018, https://psmag.com/education/the-radical-compassion-of-frederick-douglass/.

2. In-person interview with Marissa Burt, November 2023. All personal details have been removed in the interest of anonymity.

3. "Our Journey," Growing Families, accessed August 28, 2024, https://growingfamilies.life/about-us.. The Ezzos describe the origins slightly differently in the 1988 edition of *Growing Kids God's Way.*

4. Kathleen Terner and Elliot Miller, "More Than a Parenting Ministry: The Cultic Characteristics of Growing Families International," *Christian Research Journal* (Spring 1998): 2, http://www.ezzo.info/Aney/crjpartone.pdf. Here is a summary from their own website: "The *Growing Kids God's Way* Series 5th edition (1996) DVDs and Workbook was the first major parenting course written for the Christian community and has since served over two million households. While the years have passed, and fashions have changed, the principles contained within remain timeless." Gary and Anne Marie Ezzo, "Overview of Course," Growing Families, accessed September 20, 2024, https://growingfamilies.life/growing-kids-gods-way.

5. Letters from Grace Community Church and Living Hope Evangelical Fellowship, "Timeline," Ezzo.Info, 2015, http://www.ezzo.info/top-resources/top-timeline.

6. Ezzo.Info, a watchdog website, claims that both adult daughters have cut off contact with their parents. Anne Marie also blogged about keeping special memories for grandchildren she was unable to see. "Open Letter," Ezzo.Info, 2006, accessed September 27, 2024, http://www.ezzo.info/Articles/openletter.htm; and Anne Marie Ezzo, "Notes to Our Little Friends," Anne Marie's Journal, 2006, https://web.archive.org/web/20061215182739/http://www.garyezzo.net:80/LittleFriends_Journal.aspx.

7. Matthew Aney, "'Baby wise' Advice Linked to Dehydration, Failure to Thrive," *AAP News* 14, no. 4 (1998): 21, https://publications.aap.org/aapnews/article-abstract/14/4/21/17282.

8. Fight, Laugh & Feast Network, Prodigal America Conference Sponsorship, accessed March 31, 2025, https://flfnetwork.com/sponsorship-conference-information/.

9. The challenges of BIPOC authors and publishing professionals in the religion sector have been reported by *Publishers Weekly*, which noted in 2022 that in the industry broadly, 84 percent of salaried employees were White. See Cathy Lynn Grossman, "How Religion Publishing Became a Billion-Dollar Business," *Publishers Weekly*, April 19, 2022, https://www.publishersweekly.com/pw/by-topic/industry-news/religion/article/89000-how-religion-publishing-became-a-billion-dollar-industry.html. Like the American evangelical church, the evangelical publishing sector has historically been predominantly White, both in terms of authors and industry professionals. See Ann Byle, "Agents Speak on the State of BIPOC Representation in Christian Books," *Publishers Weekly*, October 2, 2024, https://www.publishersweekly.com/pw/by-topic/industry-news/religion/article/96081-agents-speak-on-the-state-of-bipoc-representation-in-christian-books.html. For explorations of the history of racial segregation and discrimination in American evangelicalism, see Anthea Butler, *White Evangelical Racism: The Politics of Morality in America* (University of North Carolina Press, 2021); and Jesse Curtis, *The Myth of Colorblind Christians: Evangelicals and White Supremacy in the Civil Rights Era* (New York University Press, 2021).

10. Gary and Anne Marie Ezzo, *Growing Kids God's Way: Reaching the Heart of Your Child With a God-Centered Purpose* (Growing Families International, 2007), 31.

11. Emily Jensen and Laura Wifler, *Risen Motherhood* (Harvest House, 2019), 13.

Chapter 1 The Right Kind of Parents

1. *The Music Man*, music and lyrics by Meredith Willson (1957).

2. Marcia Bunge, ed., *The Child in Christian Thought* (Eerdmans, 2001), 10–26. See also Jerome W. Berryman, *Children and the Theologians: Clearing the Way for Grace* (Morehouse Publishing, 2009).

3. St. Augustine, *Confessions*, trans. John Rotelle (Augustinian Heritage Institute, 1997), 46.

4. Cotton Mather, *Cares About the Nurseries: Two Brief Discourses* (T. Green, 1702).

5. Charles Wallace Jr., ed., *Susanna Wesley: The Complete Writings* (Oxford University Press, 1997), 369–73.

6. These publishers are referred to here as "evangelical" because they were Protestants producing tracts and Bibles for ministries like the American Bible Society. They sought to appeal to audiences across Protestant denominations, often stemming from concerns about the growing Catholic population. See Daniel Vaca, *Evangelicals Incorporated: Books and the Business of Religion in America* (Harvard University Press, 2019), 25–27.

7. Vaca, *Evangelicals Incorporated*, 27.

8. Vaca, *Evangelicals Incorporated*, 29.

9. For a history of the Sunday school movement, see Stephen Orchard and John Briggs, eds., *The Sunday School Movement: Studies in the Growth and Decline of Sunday Schools* (Wipf & Stock, 2007).

10. "Editor's Note," *The Mother's Assistant and Young Lady's Friend*, June 1849, i (emphasis in original).

11. Jacob Abbott, "Cautions and Counsels to Parents," *The Mother's Assistant and Young Lady's Friend*, June 1849, 1.

12. The emergence of the concept of childhood has been traced in a number of scholarly works, perhaps most notably Philippe Ariè, *Centuries of Childhood: A Social History of Family Life* (J. Cape, 1973).

13. *Children: The Magazine for Parents*, October 1926, 1, https://www.google.com/books/edition/Children/KxrTAAAAMAAJ.

14. Peter Stearns, *Anxious Parents: A History of Modern Childrearing in America* (New York University Press, 2003), 1.

15. Stearns, *Anxious Parents*, 2.

16. G. K. Chesterton, "The Fallacy of Success," in *All Things Considered* (John Lane Company, 1913), 21.

17. Chesterton, "Fallacy of Success," 26.

18. Jessica Lamb-Shapiro, "A Short History of Self-Help, the World's Best-Selling Genre," *Publishing Perspectives*, November 29, 2013, https://publishingperspectives.com/2013/11/a-short-history-of-self-help-the-worlds-bestselling-genre.

19. Ann Hulbert, *Raising America: Experts, Parents, and a Century of Advice About Children* (Vintage Books, 2004), 13.

20. Ruth Graham, "The Rise and Fall of Baby Einstein," Slate, December 19, 2017, https://slate.com/technology/2017/12/the-rise-and-fall-of-baby-einstein.html.

21. Graham, "Rise and Fall of Baby Einstein."

22. Quoted in Hilde Løvdal Stephens, *Family Matters: James Dobson and Focus on the Family's Crusade for the Christian Home* (University of Alabama Press, 2019), 1.

23. James Dobson, *Family Under Fire* (Beacon Hill, 1976), 8.

24. James Dobson, *Dare to Discipline* (Tyndale, 1970), 1.

25. Later on, in the fifth edition of *Baby and Child Care*, Spock explicitly condemned the practice of spanking, but in the original edition he was more sympathetic to the practice. "Parents and Experts Split on Spanking," *New York Times*, June 19, 1985, C9.

26. Dobson, *Dare to Discipline*, 10–11.

27. Dobson, *Dare to Discipline*, 11.

28. Steven Mintz, *Huck's Raft: A History of American Childhood* (Belknap, 2004), 267.

29. Dobson, *Dare to Discipline*, 100.

30. Audrey Clare Farley, "The Eugenics Roots of Evangelical Family Values," *Religion & Politics*, May 12, 2021, https://arcmag.org/the-eugenics-roots-of-evangelical-family-values/.

31. David Popenoe, "Remembering My Father: An Intellectual Portrait of 'The Man Who Saved Marriages,'" Institute for American Values, November 1991, 8, https://web.archive.org/web/20210625201721/https://americanvalues.org/catalog/pdfs/wp-10.pdf.

32. Dobson, *Dare to Discipline*, 10.

33. Kristin Kobes Du Mez, *Jesus and John Wayne: How White Evangelicals Corrupted a Faith and Fractured a Nation* (Liveright, 2020), 81.

34. Stephens, *Family Matters*, 4. See also Susan Ridgely, *Practicing What the Doctor Preached* (Oxford University Press, 2017). Ridgely notes that Dobson's audience included Catholics, mainline Protestants, and evangelicals who shared certain commitments to Scripture and a conservative worldview but were not united in their embrace of the label "evangelical" and had widely varied faith practices.

35. Wendy Murray Zoba, "Daring to Discipline America," *Christianity Today*, March 1, 1999, https://www.christianitytoday.com/1999/03/daring-to-discipline-america.

Chapter 2 The Bible Tells Us So

1. Lisa Ronsick (@mountain.motherhood), "God calls us to exercise authority," Instagram, February 22, 2024, https://www.instagram.com/reel/C3qohVwSpmv.

2. Hilde Løvdal Stephens, *Family Matters: James Dobson and Focus on the Family's Crusade for the Christian Home* (University of Alabama Press, 2019), 1.

3. Jason Blakely, *Lost in Ideology: Interpreting Modern Political Life* (Agenda Publishing, 2024), 1.

4. This is derived from the definition of "influencer" used by Sara Petersen in her book, *Momfluenced: Inside the Maddening, Picture-Perfect World of Mommy Influencer Culture* (Beacon, 2023): "Someone who commodifies a lifestyle or an identity for the purposes of selling something, whether that something is a product or an idea or a belief or a way of being" (4).

5. J. I. Packer, *Beyond the Battle for the Bible*, quoted in Molly Worthen, *Apostles of Reason: The Crisis of Authority in American Evangelicalism* (Oxford University Press, 2013), 200.

6. Scott Coley refers to this as "commonsense-ism": when evangelical leaders claim that Scripture's meaning and intended purpose are self-evident and plainly available to the reader. Coley points out the impossibility of this approach, since anyone can claim *their* reading is in fact the one that any reader with true common sense would agree with. See Scott M. Coley, *Ministers of Propaganda: Truth, Power, and the Ideology of the Religious Right* (Eerdmans, 2024), 19.

7. From the Greek *noutheteō*, which means "to admonish."

8. Larry Christenson, *The Christian Family* (Bethany House, 1970), 13 (emphasis original).

9. Richard Luscombe, "Tucker Carlson Warms Up Crowd With Bizarre Spanking Rant," *The Guardian*, October 24, 2024, https://www.theguardian.com/us-news/2024/oct/24/tucker-carlson-trump-rally-spanking.

10. James Dobson, *Family Under Fire* (Beacon Hill, 1976).

11. "Today's Youth: The Great Generation," NBC Radio, October 16, 1968. Transcript available at https://www.presidency.ucsb.edu/documents/remarks-the-nbc-radio-network-todays-youth-the-great-generation.

12. See Kristin Kobes Du Mez, *Jesus and John Wayne: How White Evangelicals Corrupted a Faith and Fractured a Nation* (Liveright, 2020); Michael W. Flamm, *Law and Order: Street Crime, Civil Unrest, and the Crisis of Liberalism in the 1960s* (Columbia University Press, 2005); Ruth Murray Brown, *For a "Christian America": A History of the Religious Right* (Prometheus Books, 2002); Seth Dowland, "'Family Values' and the Formation of a Christian Right Agenda," *Church History* 78, no 3 (2009): 606–31, https://doi.org.10.1017/S0009640709990448; Daniel K. Williams, *God's Own Party: The Making of the Christian Right* (Oxford University Press, 2010); and Coley, *Ministers of Propaganda*.

13. In 1995, LaHaye claimed to have conducted nine hundred seminars in forty-six countries and reached a million people. Tim and Beverly LaHaye, *The Spirit-Filled Family* (Thomas Nelson, 1995), 10.

14. Tim LaHaye, *The Battle for the Family* (Revell, 1982), i.

15. Christenson, *Christian Family*, 198, 199.

16. For a history of the Lutheran renewal movement, see Robert Longman, "Lutheran Charismatics—Renewal or Schism?," in *Lutherans Today: American Lutheran Identity in the Twenty-First Century*, ed. Richard Cimino (Eerdmans, 2003), 125–39.

17. Christenson, *Christian Family*, 212.

18. Kenneth O. Gangel, *The Family First: Biblical Answers to Family Questions* (BMH Books, 1972), 10.

19. Gangel, *Family First*, 7.

20. Gangel, *Family First*, 130.

21. Margaret L. Bendroth, *Growing Up Protestant: Parents, Children, and Mainline Churches* (Rutgers University Press, 2002), 3.

22. Ralph Mattson and Thom Black, *Discovering Your Child's Design* (David C. Cook, 1989), 20.

23. "Q&A Panel–For the Valley, with Jonny Ardavanis, Costi Hinn, John MacArthur, Scott Ardavanis," YouTube video, posted by Grace Church, April 20, 2024, 36:27, https://www.youtube.com/watch?v=SV9Io7r_hGw.

24. Abbie Halberstadt, *M Is for Mama: A Rebellion Against Mediocre Motherhood* (Harvest House, 2022), 8, 9.

25. M Is for Mama podcast webpage, accessed March 31, 2025, https://podcasts.apple.com/us/podcast/m-is-for-mama-podcast/id1664528555.

26. Abbie Halberstadt (@m.is.for.mama), "Someone in my weekly Q&A," Instagram, November 4, 2024, https://www.instagram.com/p/DB-Pd3QRH69/.

27. Wholesome Homefront (@whole.homefront), "What an ultra-crunchy," Instagram, November 13, 2024, https://www.instagram.com/p/DCVOibhyXly/.

28. Share the Arrows event page at https://www.sharethearrows.com.

29. Anne Hulbert, *Raising America: Experts, Parents, and a Century of Advice About Children* (Vintage Books, 2003).

30. William Sears, a self-identified evangelical Christian, is credited with popularizing "attachment parenting" with his bestseller *The Baby Book* (Little, Brown and Company, 1992). We haven't devoted time to discussing attachment parenting because while Sears himself was a Christian, he did not market attachment parenting as a "Christian" approach to parenting, nor did he position himself as a faith leader in most of his public-facing work.

31. Petersen, *Momfluenced*, 9–10.

32. Kate Bowler, *The Preacher's Wife: The Precarious Power of Evangelical Women Celebrities* (Princeton University Press, 2019).

33. Risen Motherhood closed in April 2025, citing—among other things—that they themselves had moved on in their parenting lives to parent teenagers and young adults. Risen Motherhood, "What's Next for Risen Motherhood—Why We're Calling Year 10 Our Last," Risen Motherhood, May 22, 2024, https://www.risenmotherhood.com/articles/whats-next-for-risen-motherhood-why-were-calling-year-10-our-last.

34. Sociologists and media scholars have explored the ways race shapes the influencer landscape. See, for example, Angèle Christin and Yingdan Lu, "The Influencer Pay Gap: Platform Labor Meets Racial Capitalism," *New Media & Society* 26, no. 12 (2023), https://doi.org/10.1177/14614448231164995; and Megan Rim, "Race, Gender, and Visibility on Social Media," in *Technology Ethics*, ed. Gregory J. Robson and Johnathan Y. Tsou (Routledge, 2023).

Chapter 3 Umbrellas of Authority

1. Tedd Tripp, *Shepherding a Child's Heart* (Shepherd, 1995), 138.

2. Gary and Anne Marie Ezzo, *Growing Kids God's Way: Reaching the Heart of Your Child With a God-Centered Purpose* (Growing Families International, 2007), 34.

3. "[Augustine] believed that the taint [of original sin] was propagated from parent to child by the physical act of generation, or rather as the result of the carnal excitement which accompanied it . . . in the sexual intercourse even of baptized persons." J. N. D. Kelly, *Early Christian Doctrines* (HarperOne, 1978), 363.

4. See Danielle Treweek, *The Meaning of Singleness: Retrieving an Eschatological Vision for the Contemporary Church* (IVP Academic, 2023), for numerous examples of contemporary pastor-teachers elevating the married state.

5. This vision was formulated as a direct response to egalitarianism. See "The Danvers Statement," The Council on Biblical Manhood and Womanhood, accessed September 14, 2024, https://cbmw.org/about/the-danvers-statement.

6. John Piper and Wayne Grudem, eds., *Recovering Biblical Manhood and Womanhood: A Response to Evangelical Feminism* (Crossway, 1991).

7. Piper and Grudem, *Recovering Biblical Manhood and Womanhood*, 350.

8. James Dobson, *Straight Talk to Men: Recovering the Biblical Meaning of Manhood* (Word, 1995), 93.

9. Justin Charles, Zoom interview with Marissa Burt, August 16, 2024.

10. Prior to the 1990s and 2000s, most mainstream resources addressed parenting in general. A few, like Dobson's *Preparing for Adolescence* (1980) and Josh McDowell's *Why Wait?* (1987), discussed the differences between boys and girls, but these were concerned primarily with sexual abstinence rather than teaching parents how to "successfully" raise boys and girls.

11. Joseph Nicolosi, *Preventing Homosexuality: A Parent's Guide*, quoted in James Dobson, *Bringing Up Boys: Practical Advice and Encouragement for Those Shaping the Next Generation of Men* (Tyndale, 2001), 120.

12. Dobson, *Bringing Up Boys*, 128.

13. Dobson, *Bringing Up Boys*, 120. Dobson presents as authoritative the work of NARTH (National Association for Research and Therapy of Homosexuality) and that of Robert Spitzer, John Paulk, and George Rekers, men who were controversial and staunch supporters of conversion therapy.

Spitzer later retracted his position and issued an apology. Paulk, who was put on leave at Focus on the Family after being caught at a gay bar, disavowed his belief in conversion therapy and also issued a formal apology. Rekers resigned from NARTH when he made headlines over allegations of an inappropriate relationship with a man he met on the Rentboy website. Exodus International, the primary organization Dobson recommends in his book for conversion therapy, shut its doors and also apologized. The 2010 audio version of *Bringing Up Boys* has removed the reference to Rekers without commentary, but a spokesperson from Focus on the Family confirmed that the book has not been updated. Brad Mazzocco, email, December 4, 2024.

14. Douglas Wilson, *Future Men: Raising Boys to Fight Giants* (Canon, 2012), 13–18.

15. See https://cinemaofwonder.com for an archived collection of Vision Forum catalogs and content, and http://www.operationmeatball.com for the ministry started by Phillips's adult children that relies on live action role playing of World War II battles.

16. Wilson, *Future Men*, 20–21.

17. Douglas LeBlanc, "Wildheart," *Christianity Today*, August 2004, https://www.christianitytoday.com/2004/08/wildheart/. Eldredge makes this comment in his Wild at Heart video series.

18. "Mark Driscoll Says Just Grow Up," *Relevant*, September 9, 2010, https://relevantmagazine.com/faith/mark-driscoll-says-just-grow/.

19. Elizabeth George, *A Woman After God's Own Heart* (Harvest House, 1997), 87.

20. Theologian Emily Hunter McGowin explains how these cultural practices were presented to evangelical women as part of God's divine design, something that resulted in men being perceived as "guardians of religion and morality" while women were encouraged to retreat from the public sphere entirely—without even the activism and volunteerism that were once available to Victorian women. See Emily Hunter McGowin, *Quivering Families: The Quiverfull Movement and Evangelical Theology of the Family* (Fortress, 2018), 17.

21. Piper and Grudem, *Recovering Biblical Manhood and Womanhood*, 366.

22. Piper and Grudem, *Recovering Biblical Manhood and Womanhood*, 376. Dorothy Patterson's chapter (along with those of Paige Patterson and George Rekers) were excised from later editions of the book.

23. BIPOC perspectives are nearly absent from most evangelical parenting resources. Many White evangelicals resist discussions surrounding White supremacy in American history, something that may keep them ignorant to the fact that Christians have advocated for certain familial ideals (e.g., White European domestic life) while also supporting economic or political approaches that expressly withhold that ideal from others. For example, Heather Williams explains how enslaved people were separated from spouses and parents and how their "obligation to provide labor for an owner took precedence over [an enslaved person's] personal needs," including family relationships. Heather Andrea Williams, "How Slavery Affected African American Families," TeacherServe, National Humanities Center, accessed September 16, 2024, https://nationalhumanitiescenter.org/education-material/how-slavery-affected-african-american-families.

Additionally, chattel slavery and other staples of American economic life, like indentured servitude, an economy built on child labor, and exploitative working hours at mills and factories, subsidized the achievement of what *became* the Christian ideal of family life for a select few: a nuclear family who owns or rents their own home, a father who goes out and earns a paycheck to "provide," a mother who keeps house and tends to children and her husband, a happy mythical picture that centers around middle-class Victorian aspirations. For more on how ideals about home are anachronistic, see Judith Flanders, *The Making of Home: The 500-Year Story of How Our Houses Became Our Homes* (Thomas Dunne Books, 2014).

24. *Read the Room: A Worldview Guide to Interior Design*, hosted by Rebekah Merkle, Canon Plus video series, 2023.

25. George, *Woman After God's Own Heart*, 68.

26. George, *Woman After God's Own Heart*, 58.

27. George, *Woman After God's Own Heart*, 58–95.

28. Christina Fox, *Idols of a Mother's Heart* (Christian Focus Publications, 2018), 36.

29. Fox, *Idols of a Mother's Heart*, 105.

30. Nancy Leigh DeMoss, ed., *Biblical Womanhood in the Home* (Crossway, 2002), 24.

31. For example, Teri Maxwell, a homeschooling mom, created resources by which women could systematize their responsibilities. She explains in multiple places how living by a schedule enabled her to continue homeschooling through twelve years of chronic debilitating depression. Teri Maxwell, "A Schedule Can Help with Depression," *Titus* 2, September 1, 2015, https://articles.titus2.com/a-schedule-can-help-with-depression.

32. Elisabeth Elliot, *The Shaping of a Christian Family* (Revell, 1992), 103.

33. Eric Metaxas, *Seven Women and the Secret of Their Greatness* (Thomas Nelson, 2015), 41.

34. Charles Wallace Jr., ed., *Susanna Wesley: The Complete Writings* (Oxford University Press, 1997), 17.

35. Many resources reference Albert E. Winship's *Jukes Edwards: A Study in Education and Heredity* (1900), available in the public domain.

36. Kenneth Minkema, "Jonathan Edwards," The Yale and Slavery Research Project, accessed September 14, 2024, https://ysrp.yale.edu/jonathan-edwards.

37. It is probable that evangelical women underreport abuse, likely due to all the teaching detailed in this chapter as well as cultural pressures against separation and divorce and methods of church discipline. For an example, see Kate Shellnut, "Grace Community Church Rejected Elder's Calls to 'Do Justice' in Abuse Case," *Christianity Today*, February 9, 2023, https://www.christianitytoday.com/2023/02/grace-community-church-elder-biblical-counseling-abuse.

38. See Sarah Stankorb, *Disobedient Women: How a Small Group of Faithful Women Exposed Abuse, Brought Down Powerful Pastors, and Ignited an Evangelical Reckoning* (Worthy Books, 2023); Christa Brown, *Baptistland: A Memoir of Abuse, Betrayal, and Transformation* (Lake Drive Books, 2024); Cait West, *Rift: A Memoir of Breaking Away from Christian Patriarchy* (Eerdmans, 2024); and Tia Levings, *A Well-Trained Wife: My Escape from Christian Patriarchy* (Macmillan, 2024).

39. "A girl who has wrestled with her father and hugged and kissed him throughout childhood can't possibly understand why he leans away now [after puberty] when she throws her arms around him. . . . His attraction to her is involuntary and usually quite innocent." James Dobson, *Bringing Up Girls: Practical Advice and Encouragement for Those Shaping the Next Generation of Women* (Tyndale, 2010), 95.

40. Voddie Baucham, "Biblical Womanhood," sermon, August 11, 2013, YouTube, 32 min., 50 sec., https://www.youtube.com/watch?v=YnLYcpLf5Zg&t=1970s, quoted in Rick Pidcock, who writes, "Plagiarism is the least thing to worry about with Voddie Baucham, who is a threat to children, women, and daughters," *Baptist News*, March 7, 2022, https://baptistnews.com/article

/plagiarism-is-the-least-thing-to-worry-about-with-voddie-baucham-who-is-a-threat-to-children-women-and-daughters/.

41. A handful of evangelical motherhood resources have a notable absence of teaching about gender hierarchy. Sally Clarkson, for example, wrote *The Mission of Motherhood* (2003) and *The Ministry of Motherhood* (2004), books that encourage women to consider Jesus's example of leadership and replicate it in their families. Gloria Furman wrote *Missional Motherhood* (2016) not to tell mothers *how* to parent but to orient their work in the overarching narrative of Scripture.

42. For critical analysis of evangelical teaching on sex and marriage, see the work of Sheila Wray Gregoire, Rebecca Gregoire Lindenbach, and Joanna Sawatsky.

43. Elisabeth Elliot explains that "in the marriage chamber, [a bride] surrenders her body, her priceless gift of virginity, all that has been hidden." She goes on to talk about how mothers surrender their own lives for the sake of their children. Elliot, "The Essence of Femininity," quoted in Piper and Grudem, *Recovering Biblical Manhood and Womanhood*, 398.

When Piper attempts to explain sexual foreplay, he reaches for this language as well: "A feminine initiation is in effect an invitation for the man to do his kind of initiating. In one sense then you could say that in those times the man is responding. But in fact, the wife is inviting him to lead in a way as only a man can, so that she can respond to him." Piper and Grudem, *Recovering Biblical Manhood and Womanhood*, 40.

44. While the Roman Catholic Church consistently rejected artificial means of contraception, the Protestant church diverged in the early 1900s, marking a new era whereby Protestant couples have widely varying practices. The Torodes sourced Roman Catholic teaching to advocate for an unrestrained openness to children unless serious circumstances required prevention via natural family planning.

45. See Joshua Harris, "A Statement on *I Kissed Dating Goodbye*," joshharris.com, accessed September 16, 2024. The Torodes first issued a statement clarifying their stance (Bethany Torode, "An Update from Bethany," May 2006, https://web.archive.org/web/20060619213236/http://www.openembrace.com/). Sam Torode then asked their publisher to discontinue *Open Embrace* in 2010. Mark Oppenheimer, "An Evolving View of Natural Family Planning," *New York Times*, July 8, 2011, https://www.nytimes.com/2011/07/09/us/09beliefs.html.

46. Infertility and adoption may be discussed in spiritual terms, but most authors write from a perspective that assumes their readers have already given birth to children. Women will often identify themselves by their number of children, including babies that were lost to miscarriage. Adoption is sometimes paired with missional, evangelistic, or ministry-oriented goals. See Kathryn Joyce, "Orphan Fever: The Evangelical Movement's Adoption Obsession," Mother Jones, May/June 2013, https://www.motherjones.com/politics/2013/04/christian-evangelical-adoption-liberia/.

47. "The Church in Exile vs. The Church Conquest," by Joel Webbon, April 16, 2023, Right Response Ministries, 18 min., 45 sec., https://rightresponse ministries.com/sermons/series/joshua/the-church-in-exile-vs-the-church-con quest/.

48. Martha Peace, *The Excellent Wife: A Biblical Perspective* (Focus Publishing, 1999), 239.

49. Daniel A. Cox and Kelsey Eyre Hammond, "Young Women Are Leaving Church in Unprecedented Numbers," American Survey Center, April 4, 2024, https://www.americansurveycenter.org/newsletter/young-women-are -leaving-church-in-unprecedented-numbers/.

Chapter 4 Who's In Charge Here?

1. Elizabeth Krueger, *Raising Godly Tomatoes: Loving Parenting with Only Occasional Trips to the Woodshed* (Krueger Publishing, 2007), 21.

2. James Dobson, "Why I Use Fighting Words," *Christianity Today*, June 19, 1995. In this op-ed, Dobson responds to criticism about his use of militant language in books like *Children at Risk* (Word, 1990).

3. James Dobson, *The Strong-Willed Child: Birth Through Adolescence* (Tyndale, 1985), 7. Dobson's observation is similar in many ways to the posting of videos or anecdotes of misbehaving children online. Most Christian parenting teachers either dismiss or ignore the reality that neurodivergence and disability can impact child behavior. Some, like Dobson, even caution that parents of "sick or deformed" children are "likely to find discipline harder to implement," and they should make every effort not to shy away from discipline because "the need to be controlled and governed is almost universal in childhood." James Dobson, *Dare to Discipline* (Tyndale, 1970), 39.

4. Dobson, *Strong-Willed Child*, 18.

5. Michael Flamm, *Law and Order: Street Crime, Civil Unrest, and the Crisis of Liberalism in the 1960s* (Columbia University Press, 2005), 3.

6. Douglas Wilson recounts this anecdote in *Why Children Matter* (Canon, 2018), 121. Rachel Jankovic produces parenting content for Canon Press.

7. Dobson, *Strong-Willed Child*, 45 (emphasis in original).

8. Dobson suggests that "mild" spankings can begin between fifteen and eighteen months of age. Dobson, *Strong-Willed Child*, 46.

9. Dobson, *Strong-Willed Child*, 47.

10. Dobson, *Strong-Willed Child*, 47.

11. David Wilkerson, *The Cross and the Switchblade: A True Story of the Saving Power of Faith* (Hodder & Stoughton, 1963).

12. Larry Christenson, *The Christian Family* (Bethany House, 1970), 116–17.

13. Kenneth O. Gangel, *The Family First: Biblical Answers to Family Questions* (BMH Books, 1972), 63.

14. James Dobson, *Parenting Isn't for Cowards: Dealing Confidently with the Frustrations of Child-Rearing* (Word, 1987), 14 (emphasis in original).

15. Bruce Narramore, *An Ounce of Prevention: A Parent's Guide to Moral and Spiritual Growth in Children* (Zondervan, 1973), 12.

16. Narramore, *Ounce of Prevention*, 11.

17. Narramore, *Ounce of Prevention*, 11.

18. James Dobson, *Dare to Discipline* (Tyndale, 1970), 28.

19. Bruce Ray, *Withhold Not Correction* (Presbyterian and Reformed, 1978), 31 (emphasis in original).

20. Tim Kimmel, *Legacy of Love: A Plan for Parenting on Purpose* (Multnomah, 1989), 13 (emphasis in original).

21. Douglas Wilson, *Standing on the Promises* (Canon, 1997), 44–45.

22. Canon Press email advertisement, November 16, 2023.

23. Douglas Wilson, "Yeah, That Was Really Bad," Blog & Mablog, November 17, 2023, https://dougwils.com/books-and-culture/s7-engaging-the-culture/yeah-that-was-really-bad.html.

24. John Rosemond, *Parenting by the Book: Biblical Wisdom for Raising Your Child* (Howard Books, 2007), 178, 182.

25. Margie and Gregg Lewis, *The Hurting Parent: Help and Hope for Parents of Prodigals* (Zondervan, 1980), 9–10.

26. Chuck Swindoll, *The Strong Family: Growing Wise in Family Life* (Multnomah, 1991), 174 (emphasis in original).

27. Swindoll, *Strong Family*, 174.

28. Swindoll, *Strong Family*, 182 (emphasis in original).

29. Swindoll, *Strong Family*, 182.

Chapter 5 Are Children Human?

1. "The Top 50 Books That Have Shaped Evangelicals," *Christianity Today*, October 2006, https://www.christianitytoday.com/2006/10/top-50-books-that-have-shaped-evangelicals/.

2. Henry Cloud and John Townsend, *Boundaries with Kids: When to Say Yes, When to Say No, to Help Your Children Gain Control of Their Lives* (Zondervan, 1998), 9.

3. Cloud and Townsend, *Boundaries with Kids*, 10.

4. James Dobson, *Dare to Discipline* (Tyndale, 1970), 14.

5. Tedd Tripp, *Shepherding a Child's Heart* (Shepherd, 1995), 48–49.

6. Larry Christenson, *The Christian Family* (Bethany House, 1970), 57.

7. Nicholas Wolterstorff, *Journey Toward Justice: Personal Encounters in the Global South* (Baker Academic, 2013), 157–58.

8. Bonnie Miller-McLemore, *Let the Children Come: Reimagining Childhood from a Christian Perspective* (Fortress, 2019), xxviii.

9. Cloud and Townsend, *Boundaries with Kids*, 119.

10. Cloud and Townsend, *Boundaries with Kids*, 44.

11. Stacey Manning and Katy Faust argue in their recent book *Them Before Us: Why We Need a Global Children's Rights Movement* (Post Hill Press, 2021) that children have a right to be raised by two parents—a mother

and a father, specifically—and the right not to be subjected to particular kinds of gender-affirming care.

12. For a quick overview of the idea at work here, see Joe Rigney, "The Enticing Sin of Empathy: How Satan Corrupts Through Compassion," Desiring God, May 31, 2019, https://www.desiringgod.org/articles/the-enticing-sin-of-empathy.

13. Ken Ham and Steve Ham, *Raising Godly Children in an Ungodly World: Leaving a Lasting Legacy* (Master Books, 2006), 179.

14. Ham and Ham, *Raising Godly Children*, 184.

15. Ham and Ham, *Raising Godly Children*, 182 (emphasis in original).

16. Ham and Ham, *Raising Godly Children*, 184.

17. Ham and Ham, *Raising Godly Children*, 184.

18. Ham and Ham, *Raising Godly Children*, 180.

19. Voddie Baucham, "Vipers in Diapers," posted June 9, 2019, by Gospel Partners Media/Wretched, YouTube, 1 min., 30 sec., https://www.youtube.com/watch?v=deQWcXYsu1M.

Voddie goes on to describe a child's cries of defiance and stiffening of their body as evidence of their depravity, joking that God makes children small so they can't kill their parents, and he makes them cute so their parents won't kill them. For further exploration of this imagery, see R. L. Stollar, "The Child as Viper: How Voddie Baucham's Theology of Children Promotes Abuse," Homeschoolers Anonymous, January 16, 2015, https://homeschoolersanonymous.net/2015/01/16/the-child-as-viper-how-voddie-bauchams-theology-of-children-promotes-abuse/.

20. James Dobson, *The Strong-Willed Child: Birth Through Adolescence* (Tyndale, 1985), 37.

21. Dorothy L. Sayers, *Are Women Human? Astute and Witty Essays on the Role of Women in Society* (1971; repr., Eerdmans, 2005), 24.

22. Chuck Swindoll, *The Strong Family: Growing Wise in Family Life* (Multnomah, 1991), 182 (emphasis removed).

23. Nadya Williams, *Mothers, Children, and the Body Politic: Ancient Christianity and the Recovery of Human Dignity* (IVP Academic, 2024), 109.

24. Rebekah Mui, founding editor of the online publication *The Kingdom Outpost*, explains how evangelical family teaching relies on imperial masculinity: "Children were viewed much like slaves in the Roman Empire and were controlled through bodily domination and penetration." Zoom interview with Marissa Burt, August 31, 2024.

25. R. L. Stollar, *The Kingdom of Children: A Liberation Theology* (Eerdmans, 2023), 106.

26. See Philip Greven, *Spare the Child: The Religious Roots of Punishment and the Psychological Impact of Physical Abuse* (Knopf, 1990); and Alice Miller, *For Your Own Good: Hidden Cruelty in Child-Rearing and the Roots of Violence* (Farrar, Straus & Giroux, 1980).

27. This belief that if parents fail to punish, then they themselves will be subject to punishment is pervasive in Christian teaching. Christenson says as

much in *The Christian Family*: "God holds you accountable for the discipline of your children. If you discipline and bring up your children according to His Word, you will have His approval and blessing. If you fail to do so, you will incur His wrath" (91).

28. Stollar, *Kingdom of Children*, 106.

29. Christian leaders, including Dorothy Patterson, John MacArthur, and others, have appealed to Isaiah 3:12, "Youths oppress my people, women rule over them," to argue that child-centric considerations (as well as feminism) are markers of divine judgment on American society.

30. Heather Creekmore, "My Biggest Parenting Regret: Baby Wise," Dallas Moms, November 7, 2013, https://dallasmoms.com/my-biggest-parenting-regret-babywise/comment-page-6/.

31. Steven Mintz, *Huck's Raft: A History of American Childhood* (Harvard Belknap, 2004), 345.

32. Bruce Narramore, *An Ounce of Prevention: A Parent's Guide to Moral and Spiritual Growth in Children* (Zondervan, 1972), 16.

33. S. Bruce Narramore, *No Condemnation: Rethinking Guilt Motivation in Preaching, Counseling, and Parenting* (1984; repr., Wipf & Stock, 2002), 24.

Chapter 6 Sinners from Their Mothers' Wombs

1. In reaction to Origen's ideas about preborn souls awaiting bodies, theologians developed counterpoints like *traducianism* (the soul is imparted by God at conception) and *creationism* (the soul is imparted directly by God to the body at some point). See Ted Nelson, "Traducianism? Creationism? What Has an Ancient Debate to Do with the Modern Debate over Abortion?," *Denison Journal of Religion* 13, no. 2 (2014), https://digitalcommons.denison.edu/cgi/viewcontent.cgi?article=1085&context=religion.

For further reading, see J. N. D. Kelly, *Early Christian Doctrines* (HarperOne, 1978), 163–88.

2. Kelly, *Early Christian Doctrines*, 176.

3. Kelly, *Early Christian Doctrines*, 179.

4. Dr. Kathleen Noll-Syrigos, email to Marissa Burt, April 2024.

5. Ginger Hubbard, *Don't Make Me Count to Three: A Mom's Look at Heart-Oriented Discipline* (Shepherd, 2003), 29–30.

6. Hubbard, *Don't Make Me Count to Three*, 29.

7. J. Richard Fugate, *What the Bible Says About Child Training: Parenting with Confidence* (Foundation for Biblical Research, 1980), 62.

8. Fugate, *What the Bible Says*, 63.

9. Bruce Ray, *Withhold Not Correction* (Presbyterian and Reformed, 1978), 28.

10. Baptized infants would later be *confirmed* in the faith. Adult converts were, in baptism, washed clean of original sin as well as previous acts of sin. This historic practice contrasts with the (relatively) newer practice of

"believer's baptism," whereby people receive baptism only after coming to a cognitive understanding and acceptance of faith.

11. Ray rejects the idea of an age of accountability outright and instead employs a kind of circular reasoning: "If, again, we presuppose that children are by nature *innocent* (without guilt or personal sin) until they reach some rather vague *age of accountability*, then how can we account for the anger, frustration, and selfishness that are apparent even from the earliest days?" Ray, *Withhold Not Correction*, 13 (emphasis in original).

12. Jonathan Edwards, "Sinners in the Hands of an Angry God," sermon preached in Enfield, Connecticut, July 8, 1741. The text of the sermon can be found at https://www.jonathan-edwards.org/Sinners.pdf.

13. Michael and Debi Pearl, *To Train Up a Child: Child Training for the 21st Century* (No Greater Joy Ministries, 1994), 18–29.

14. Tedd Tripp, *Shepherding a Child's Heart* (Shepherd, 1995), 152.

15. Tripp, *Shepherding a Child's Heart*, 6.

16. Tripp, *Shepherding a Child's Heart*, 29.

17. In the resources Gothard created for hundreds of thousands of families, parents and children together learned definitions for common character qualities that were all linked to a reinforcing Scripture reference. Jeri, "Character First and Bill Gothard," *Heresy in the Heartland* (blog), September 28, 2013, https://heresyintheheartland.blogspot.com/2013/09/character-first-and-bill-gothard.html.

18. Ginger Hubbard, host, *Parenting with Ginger Hubbard*, podcast, episode 1, "How It All Began (Part 1)," February 1, 2021, https://www.gingerhubbard.com/blogs/podcast/parenting-with-ginger-hubbard-how-it-all-began-part-1; and episode 2, "How It All Began (Part 2)," February 1, 2021, https://www.gingerhubbard.com/blogs/podcast/parenting-with-ginger-hubbard-how-it-all-began-part-2.

19. Ginger Hubbard, *Wise Words for Moms* (Shepherd, 2001), 2–3.

20. Hubbard, *Wise Words for Moms*, 5.

21. Additional Bible verses offered for whining are Prov. 25:28; Gal. 5:22–23; Eph. 4:29; 2 Pet. 1:5–8. It's important to note that no explanation or discussion of the context for these verses is given.

22. Hubbard, *Don't Make Me Count to Three*, 70–71.

23. Tripp, *Shepherding a Child's Heart*, 165–69.

24. Tripp, *Shepherding a Child's Heart*, 165–69.

25. Cornelius Plantinga Jr., *Not the Way It's Supposed to Be: A Breviary of Sin* (Eerdmans, 1995), 14.

26. John MacArthur, *What the Bible Says About Parenting: God's Plan for Rearing Your Child* (Thomas Nelson, 2000), 48.

27. Tripp, *Shepherding a Child's Heart*, 175.

28. Martha Peace and Stuart Scott, *The Faithful Parent: A Biblical Guide to Raising a Family* (P&R, 2010), 22–23.

29. For further reading on various biblical motifs for the atonement, see Fleming Rutledge, *The Crucifixion: Understanding the Death of Jesus Christ* (Eerdmans, 2015).

30. Andrew Remington Rillera argues that "the practice and logic of OT sacrifice *has nothing to do with substitution, retribution, or punishment* (i.e., *negative* retribution)." *Lamb of the Free: Recovering the Varied Sacrificial Understandings of Jesus's Death* (Cascade, 2024), 333 (emphasis in original). Rillera's work spotlights how the scapegoat that decontaminates the community from sin is not sacrificed at all; additionally, he offers careful analysis of how atonement sacrifices aren't killed on the altar but are consumed as a shared meal before the Lord—language redolent of the Eucharistic feast. Douglas A. Campbell, writing in the foreword to Rillera's book, notes the relevance to parenting: "This authoritarian model authorizes the arrangement of families in hierarchical terms and permits parents to enforce its principles. Indeed, more than this, they *ought* to. Punitive parenting will be the result, sometimes in defense of a hierarchical family order. And those who do *not* parent punitively and order their families hierarchically are doing their children a disservice as they violate the basic order of the cosmos" (xix, emphasis in original).

Chapter 7 Spare the Rod

1. See Elizabeth T. Gershoff, "Report on Physical Punishment in the United States: What Research Tells Us About Its Effects on Children," Report from the Center for Effective Discipline, Columbus, OH, 2008.

2. Aniya Greene-Santos, "Corporal Punishment in Schools Still Legal in Many States," NEA Today, May 20, 2024, https://www.nea.org/nea-today/all-news-articles/corporal-punishment-schools-still-legal-many-states.

3. "The rate was 49% in the past year for children ages 0–9, 23% for youth 10–17, and 37% overall." David Finkelhor, Heather Turner, Brittany Kay Wormuth, et al., "Corporal Punishment: Current Rates from a National Survey," *Journal of Child and Family Studies* 28 (2019): 1991–97, https://doi.org/10.1007/s10826-019-01426-4.

4. See Erica Feucht, "Juvenile Misbehaviour in Ancient Egypt," in *History of Juvenile Delinquency*, ed. Albert G. Hess and Pricilla Clemens (Aalen, 1990), https://archiv.ub.uni-heidelberg.de/propylaeumdok/3068/1/Feucht_Juvenile_misbehavior_1990.pdf.

5. Mui explains how Roman hierarchy operated according to categories of "penetrator" and "penetrated." Children and women fell in the category of "penetrated" and were expected to remain under patriarchal control, regardless of their age. Rebekah Mui, Zoom interview with Marissa Burt, August 31, 2024.

6. See Stacey Patton, *Spare the Kids: Why Whupping Children Won't Save Black America* (Beacon, 2017), and sparethekids.com.

7. Clarissa W. Atkinson, "'Wonderful Affection': Seventeenth Century Missionaries to New France on Children and Childhood," in *The Child in Christian Thought*, ed. Marcia J. Bunge (Eerdmans, 2001), 236–38.

8. Philip Greven, *Spare the Child: The Religious Roots of Punishment and the Psychological Impact of Physical Abuse* (Knopf, 1991), 24.

9. It remains to be seen how a child who requires physical coercion due to an inability to reason will comprehend how spanking is different from hitting, but so goes the argument.

10. Reb Bradley, phone interview with Marissa Burt, August 22, 2024.

11. Jay Adams in the foreword to Bruce Ray, *Withhold Not Correction* (Presbyterian and Reformed, 1978), 9.

12. Jack Hyles, *How to Rear Children* (Hyles-Anderson, 1972), 98.

13. See Murray A. Straus and Anita K. Mathur, "Social Change and the Trends in Approval of Corporal Punishment by Parents from 1968 to 1994," in *Family Violence Against Children: A Challenge for Society*, ed. Detlev Frehsee, Wiebke Horn, and Kai-D. Bussmann (Walter de Gruyter, 1996), 91–106.

14. Roy Lessin, *Spanking: Why? When? How?* (Bethany Fellowship, 1979), 69.

15. Marcia Bunge, ed., *The Child in Christian Thought* (Eerdmans, 2001), 316.

16. Greven, *Spare the Child*, 26.

17. This anecdote from Wilkinson is found in Larry Christenson, *The Christian Family* (Dimension Books, 1970), 106–7.

18. Victor I. Vieth, "Augustine, Luther and Solomon: Providing Pastoral Guidance to Parents on the Corporal Punishment of Children," *Currents in Theology and Mission* 44, no. 3 (2017): 27, https://hfh.fas.harvard.edu/files/pik/files/augustine_luther_and_solomon-_providing_pastoral_guidance_to_parents_on_the_corporal_punishment_of_children1.pdf.

19. Greven, *Spare the Child*, 15.

20. Greven, *Spare the Child*, 85.

21. Sonya Shafer, "Habits Q&A: Consequences," Simply Charlotte Mason, February 2022, https://simplycharlottemason.com/blog/habits-q-amp-a-consequences/.

22. Greven, *Spare the Child*, 14.

23. J. C. Ryle, *The Duties of Parents: Parenting Your Children God's Way* (1888; repr., Aneko Press, 2018), 35.

24. Douglas Wilson, *Federal Husband: Covenant Headship and Christian Men* (Canon, 2004), 98.

25. Ginger Hubbard, *Don't Make Me Count to Three: A Mom's Look at Heart-Oriented Discipline* (Shepherd, 2003), 123. Hubbard draws liberally from the work of Lessin and Ray.

26. Larry Tomczak, *God, the Rod, and Your Child's Bod: The Art of Loving Correction for Christian Parents* (Power Books, 1982), 48.

27. Hubbard, *Don't Make Me Count to Three*, 108, 114.

28. Nancy Campbell, *The Power of Motherhood: What the Bible Says About Mothers* (Above Rubies, 1996), 93.

29. Doug and Nancy Wilson, "Parenting Q&A, Part II," posted November 22, 2013, by Canon Press, YouTube, 58 min., 3 sec., https://youtube.com/watch?v=7gMakXQY260.

30. Ray, *Withhold Not Correction*, 15.

31. Tomczak, *God, the Rod, and Your Child's Bod*, 118. The audio version is available as "How to Raise Respectful, Responsible and Obedient Children" at https://www.larrytomczak.com/audiobooks.

32. It is almost a given that a Christian parenting book will include some kind of joke to this effect. Tripp jokes about one of his sons having a "leather bottom" and advises that "you just want to make sure there are no comic books stuffed into the pants that would keep you from being effective." Tedd Tripp, *Shepherding a Child's Heart* (Shepherd, 1995), 147–48.

Doug Wilson stated that "even though [our toddler daughter] had done nothing exactly disobedient, she certainly was walking right down the line. She was pushing it. I remember saying to my wife that we should look for an opportunity to spank her . . . and then she danced." Wilson, *Standing on the Promises*, 131.

Ginger Hubbard titles one of her chapters "The Tailbone's Connected to the . . . Heart?" And one of her advertised topics for a conference is "The 'Bottom' Line: The Biblical Use of the Rod." Hubbard, *Don't Make Me Count to Three*, 99, 156.

33. Rachel Jankovik (@CanonPress), "Spanked kids are happy kids," Instagram, October 5, 2023, https://www.instagram.com/reel/CyBRn7-LSH6.

34. Lessin, *Spanking*, 76 (emphasis in original).

35. "Practice first on yourself (but not every time!). . . . The discipline should be sufficient so that the child is crying but not screaming in angry rage." Martha Peace and Stuart Scott, *The Faithful Parent: A Biblical Guide to Raising a Family* (P&R, 2010), 58.

36. Ray, *Withhold Not Correction*, 108.

37. "If discipline has not yielded a harvest of peace and righteousness, it is not finished. On some occasions I have had to say to our children: 'Dear, Daddy has spanked you, but you are not sweet enough yet. We are going to have to go back upstairs for another spanking.'" Tripp, *Shepherding a Child's Heart*, 149.

38. Lessin, *Spanking*, 75.

39. "I meet people all the time ya' know and they say, oh yeah, 'There have only been maybe 4 or 5 times I've ever had to spank Junior.' 'Really?' 'That's unfortunate, because unless you raised Jesus II, there were days when Junior needed to be spanked 5 times before breakfast.' . . . You just need to have an all-day session where you just wear them out and they finally decide 'you know what, things get worse when I do that.'" From the sermon "Corporal Punishment and Shyness in a Young Child," quoted in R. L. Stollar, "6 Things You Should Know About Voddie Baucham," Homeschoolers Anonymous,

December 1, 2014, https://homeschoolersanonymous.net/2014/12/01/6-things-you-should-know-about-voddie-baucham/.

40. Doug and Nancy Wilson, "Keep Your Kids," posted May 6, 2019, by Canon Press, YouTube, 38 min., 43 sec., https://www.youtube.com/watch?v=U7c_nbaXG34.

41. L. Elizabeth Krueger, *Raising Godly Tomatoes: Loving Parenting with Only Occasional Trips to the Woodshed* (Krueger Publishing, 2007), 60.

42. Douglas Wilson, *Why Children Matter* (Canon Press, 2018), 110.

43. Tripp, *Shepherding a Child's Heart*, 158–59.

44. Krueger, *Raising Godly Tomatoes*, 62. Krueger isn't alone in this. Many parenting experts underscore the importance of parents "winning."

45. Krueger, *Raising Godly Tomatoes*, 62.

46. Hubbard, *Don't Make Me Count to Three*, 30–32.

47. Ray, *Withhold Not Correction*, 87.

48. Wilson, *Why Children Matter*, 117, 119.

49. Peace and Scott, *Faithful Parent*, 59.

50. "This switch was a thin stick about eighteen inches long, one of which [my mother] kept over the door in every room in the house." Elisabeth Elliot, *The Shaping of a Christian Family* (Revell, 1992), 163.

51. "For the child less than one year old whom you are conditioning to obedience, a thump with the finger is effective, or a small, ten- to twelve-inch-long, willowy branch (stripped of any knots that might break the skin), about one-eighth inch in diameter is sufficient. . . . For the larger child that is actually spanked, a light belt or a two-foot switch is effective. Most kitchens contain a good variety of instruments in the form of wooden spoons, rubber spatulas, etc." Michael and Debi Pearl, *To Train Up a Child: Child Training for the 21st Century* (No Greater Joy Ministries, 1994), 96.

52. Gwen Shamblin, a Christian weight-loss coach, applauded a parent who "locked [her son] in [his room] from that Friday until Monday and only left him in the room with his Bible." The mother praised by Shamblin was later arrested and convicted of murdering her eight-year-old son, Josef. "'DCS, CPS Investigated' Remnant Homes Following Boy's Child-Abuse Death, Gwen Shamblin Testified," NewsChannel5, November 22, 2021, https://www.newschannel5.com/news/newschannel-5-investigates/dcs-cps-investigated-remnant-homes-following-boys-child-abuse-death-gwen-shamblin-testified.

53. See Laura Robinson, "In Bible Times They'd Break a Lamb's Leg," Not Peer Reviewed: By Laura Robinson, July 28, 2024, https://laurarbnsn.substack.com/p/in-bible-times-theyd-break-a-lambs.

54. Tripp, *Shepherding a Child's Heart*, 105.

55. John Piper, "Would Jesus Spank a Child?," Desiring God, February 16, 2009, https://www.desiringgod.org/interviews/would-jesus-spank-a-child.

56. Greven, *Spare the Child*, 119–212.

57. Elizabeth Gershoff, quoted in Diane Cole, "What Happens When a Country Bans Spanking?," NPR, October 25, 2018, https://www.npr.org

/sections/goatsandsoda/2018/10/25/660191806/what-happens-when-a-country-bans-spanking.

58. Hubbard, *Don't Make Me Count to Three*, 109.

59. Clay Clarkson, *Heartfelt Discipline: Following God's Path of Life to the Heart of Your Child* (Whole Heart Press, 2003), 189–202.

60. John Rosemond, *Parenting by the Book: Biblical Wisdom for Raising Your Child* (Howard Books, 2007), 214.

61. Jim and Lynne Jackson, Zoom interview with Marissa Burt and Kelsey McGinnis, August 14, 2024. Jim and Lynne's eBook, *Perspectives on Spanking: What Does the Bible Say About Spanking?*, informs parents about different interpretive perspectives as well as current brain research. They explain that it's often difficult for one or both parents to let go of corporal punishment, so they aim to empower parents with other tools and invite them to prioritize creating emotionally and physically safe environments for children.

Like James Dobson, whose work with troubled youth led him to promote authoritarian disciplinary measures, Jim Jackson also worked with high-risk youth. He explained how this led him away from authoritarian measures. "All the trauma and all of the figurative spankings they were getting as teenagers . . . was a sophisticated caricature . . . of what happens inside of people when they're painfully disciplined in a way that doesn't make sense to them. It doesn't draw them closer. It leads them further away from the intentions of the disciplinarian."

62. Alex Clark (host), *Culture Apothecary*, podcast, "Why 'Gentle Parenting' Should Be Avoided by Christian Moms—with M Is for Mama," interview with Abbie Halberstadt, October 19, 2023, https://podcasts.apple.com/us/podcast/why-gentle-parenting-should-be-avoided-by-christian/id1507839530?i=1000631963162.

63. Karis Kimmel Murray, *Grace Based Discipline: How to Be at Your Best When Your Kids Are at Their Worst* (Family Matters Press, 2017), 192 (emphasis in original).

64. See Clarkson, *Heartfelt Discipline*, 189–204; David and Amanda Erickson, *The Flourishing Family: A Jesus-Centered Guide to Parenting with Peace and Purpose* (Tyndale, 2024), 173–90; and William J. Webb, *Corporal Punishment in the Bible: A Redemptive-Movement Hermeneutic for Troubling Texts* (InterVarsity, 2011).

65. Reb Bradley, phone interview with Marissa Burt, August 22, 2024.

66. Pearl, *To Train Up a Child*, 33–43.

67. Kevin Hayes, "Is Conservative Christian Group, No Greater Joy Ministries, Pushing Parents to Beat Kids to Death?," CBS News, October 3, 2011, https://www.cbsnews.com/news/is-conservative-christian-group-no-greater-joy-ministries-pushing-parents-to-beat-kids-to-death/.

68. Kevin Hayes, "DA: Kevin and Elizabeth Schatz Killed Daughter with 'Religious Whips' for Mispronouncing Word," CBS News, February 22, 2010, https://web.archive.org/web/20110218205033/http://www.cbsnews.com/8301-504083_162-6009742-504083.html.

69. Lee Stoll, "Kids Testify in Parents' Murder and Abuse Trial," KIRO TV, October 29, 2013, https://www.kiro7.com/news/kids-testify-parents-murder-and-abuse-trial/246537580/.

70. See Jeff Hodson, "Did Hana's Parents 'Train' Her to Death?," *Seattle Times*, November 27, 2011, https://web.archive.org/web/20120229033208/http://seattletimes.nwsource.com/html/localnews/2016875109_hana28m.html; and Erik Eckholm, "Preaching Virtue of Spanking, Even as Deaths Fuel Debate," *New York Times*, November 6, 2011, https://www.nytimes.com/2011/11/07/us/deaths-put-focus-on-pastors-advocacy-of-spanking.html.

71. Michael Pearl (interview), "Spanking: Discipline or Abuse," posted December 1, 2011, by Anderson Cooper, YouTube, 1 min., 36 sec., https://www.youtube.com/watch?v=LlL0cgIj8ds.

72. At least once, a religious leader has been held responsible for the results of such teachings. On October 5, 1982, Stuart and Leslie Green killed their twenty-three-month-old son, Joseph Green, who had refused to apologize to the grandson of commune leader Dorothy McClellan. The Greens "paddled" their son to death over the course of two hours. After Joseph's death, "the jury . . . and the judge ultimately held Dorothy McClellan responsible for the death of the boy since she was the leader of the fundamentalist religious community and the primary advocate of corporal punishments for children." Greven, *Spare the Child*, 38–39.

73. A parent commenting on one of our Instagram posts.

74. Cole Waterman, "Michigan Church Volunteer Heads to Prison for Preying on, Habitually Spanking Boys," Newsbreak, August 12, 2024, https://www.mlive.com/news/saginaw-bay-city/2024/08/michigan-church-volunteer-heads-to-prison-for-preying-on-habitually-spanking-boys.html.

75. Waterman, "Michigan Church Volunteer Heads to Prison."

Chapter 8 The Receipt Comes Due

1. Frank J. Elgar, Peter D. Donnelly, Valerie Michaelson, et al., "Corporal Punishment Bans and Physical Fighting in Adolescents: An Ecological Study of 88 Countries," *BMJ Open* 8, no. 9 (2018), https://bmjopen.bmj.com/content/8/9/e021616.

2. Elizabeth T. Gershoff and Andrew Grogan-Kaylor, "Spanking and Child Outcomes: Old Controversies and New Meta-Analyses," *Journal of Family Psychology* 30, no. 4 (2016): 453-69, https://doi.org/10.1037/fam0000191.

3. Robert E. Larzelere, "Child Outcomes of Nonabusive and Customary Physical Punishment by Parents: An Updated Literature Review," *Clinical Child and Family Psychology Review* 3 (2000): 199–221, https://doi.org/10.1023/a:1026473020315.

4. Jorge Cuartas, David G. Weissman, Margaret A. Sheridan, et al., "Corporal Punishment and Elevated Neural Response to Threat in Children," Child Development 92, no. 3 (2021): 821–32, https://doi.org/10.1111/cdev.13565.

5. Rebekah Mui, Zoom interview with Marissa Burt, August 31, 2024. See also kingdomoutpost.org. Mui also described reading Dobson's *Preparing for Adolescence* as a factual biological explanation of gender from a doctor, leading her to believe that puberty makes girls naturally want to be a wife and mother and stay-at-home mom.

6. "Map of the 53 Countries that Ban the Corporal Punishment of Children," Brilliant Maps, March 3, 2023, https://brilliantmaps.com/corporal-punishment/.

7. Prudy Ray (@PrudyRay), "Yeah, Western Evangelical beliefs," X (formerly Twitter), May 18, 2023, 10:58 a.m., https://x.com/PrudyRay/status/1659257053674893312.

8. Reb Bradley, phone interview with Marissa Burt, August 22, 2024.

9. Abigail Schrier, *Bad Therapy: Why the Kids Aren't Growing Up* (Sentinal, 2024).

10. Cait West tells her story of being raised as a stay-at-home daughter in Vision Forum and Dominionist circles in *Rift: A Memoir of Breaking Away from Christian Patriarchy* (Eerdmans, 2024). Tia Levings tells her story of marriage, domestic violence, and motherhood set in Christian patriarchy in *A Well-Trained Wife: My Escape from Christian Patriarchy* (St. Martins, 2024).

11. Investigative journalist Sarah Stankorb spotlights the stories of survivors from many evangelical empires in *Disobedient Women: How a Small Group of Faithful Women Exposed Abuse, Brought Down Powerful Pastors, and Started an Evangelical Reckoning* (Worthy, 2023).

12. Julie Anne, "Doug Phillips: The Sex Abuse Lawsuit Conclusion and Epilogue of His Vision Forum Shipwreck," *Spiritual Sounding Board*, June 28, 2016, https://spiritualsoundingboard.com/2016/06/28/doug-phillips-the-sex-abuse-lawsuit-conclusion-and-epilogue-of-his-vision-forum-shipwreck.

13. Tomczak's response was to deny the allegations and double down. "[Tomczak] also said that as a parent he was saddened to hear of the allegations." He continues to insist that his book has helped parents around the world. Bob Smietana, "Pastor Who Pushes Corporal Punishment Accused of Abuse," Religion News Service, January 16, 2013, https://religionnews.com/2013/01/16/pastor-who-pushes-corporal-punishment-accused-of-abuse/.

14. Sarah Stankorb, "That Moscow Mood: How Much Culture War Is Too Much, for American Evangelicals?," Slate, December 2, 2023, https://slate.com/human-interest/2023/12/evangelical-church-doug-wilson-idaho-culture-war-no-quarter-november.html; and Stankorb, "Inside the Church That Preaches 'Wives Need to Be Led with a Firm Hand,'" Vice, September 28, 2021, https://www.vice.com/en/article/inside-the-church-that-preaches-wives-need-to-be-led-with-a-firm-hand/.

15. Sarah Eekhoff Zylstra, "More Women Sue Bill Gothard and IBLP, Alleging Sexual Abuse," *Christianity Today*, January 8, 2016, https://www.christianitytoday.com/2016/01/more-women-sue-bill-gothard-iblp-alleging-sexual-abuse/.

16. In 1997, John MacArthur and the board of elders at Grace Community Church formally rebuked Gary Ezzo. In 2000, another church also excommunicated him. Several critical articles were written about his teaching. See "Original Grace Church Statement Regarding GFI and Gary Ezzo," ezzo.info, http://www.ezzo.info/index-of-articles/81-timeline/175-original-grace-church-statement-regarding-gfi-and-gary-ezzo.

17. Kate Shellnutt, "Grace Community Church Rejected Elder's Calls to 'Do Justice' in Abuse Case," *Christianity Today*, February 9, 2023, https://www.christianitytoday.com/2023/02/grace-community-church-elder-biblical-counseling-abuse; and Liz Lykins, "Woman Claims John MacArthur's Grace Community Church Wrongly Disciplined and Shamed Her," The Roys Report, September 10, 2024, https://julieroys.com/woman-claims-john-macarthurs-grace-community-church-wrongly-disciplined-and-shamed-her.

18. Tedd Tripp, *Shepherding a Child's Heart* (Shepherd, 1995), 168.

19. Nancy Campbell, *The Power of Motherhood: What the Bible Says About Mothers* (Above Rubies, 1996), 1.

20. John Rosemond, *Parenting by the Book: Biblical Wisdom for Raising Your Child* (Howard Books, 2007), 233.

21. Jim and Lynne Jackson, Zoom interview with Marissa Burt and Kelsey McGinnis, August 22, 2024.

22. Mike, "Mike's Story," CFCtoo, July 1, 2022, https://www.cfctoo.com/stories/mikes-story.

23. Toby Sumpter (@TJSumpter), "It's the Lord's Day, so this morning for #spankinggate I want to talk about training kids for church," X (formerly Twitter), November 19, 2023, 7:25 a.m., https://x.com/TJSumpter/status/1726260522981773443.

24. Tomczak recollects his childhood misery of waiting to "get it" after church, so he recommends spanking during services. "In our Christian community, it is quite normal to see numbers of parents take their children outside during meetings. . . . It's amazing how quietly the children sit upon their return." Larry Tomczak, *God, the Rod, and Your Child's Bod: The Art of Loving Correction for Christian Parents* (Power Books, 1982), 115.

25. Jeff R. Temple, Hye Jeong Choi, Tyson Reuter, et al., "Childhood Corporal Punishment and Future Perpetration of Physical Dating Violence," *Journal of Pediatrics* 194 (2018): 233–37, https://doi.org/10.1016/j.jpeds.2017.10.028.

26. While we were writing this book, the Instagram account Flourishing Homes and Families posted about the negative sexual impact of spanking, and hundreds of adults responded, confirming this experience. We hope that future researchers will look at the material in this link. See Flourishing Homes and Families (@flourishinghomesandfamilies), "Spanking (CW)," Instagram, March 4, 2024, https://www.instagram.com/stories/highlights/18012029462244252.

27. Bethlehem College and Seminary social media post, "Two minutes watching this video," Facebook, September 21, 2023, https://www.facebook.com/watch/?v=845144147338237.

28. Reb Bradley, phone interview with Marissa Burt, August 22, 2024.

29. In her acknowledgments, Hubbard thanks Tedd Tripp, whose insights "form the backbone of this book. . . . My thanks to Lou Priolo, whose excellent work in *The Heart of Anger* and *Teach Them Diligently* is reflected in this book. I am also grateful for Roy Lessin. . . . Much of the wisdom I gained from you is reflected in chapters 9–12." Ginger Hubbard, *Don't Make Me Count to Three: A Mom's Look at Heart-Oriented Discipline* (Shepherd, 2003), 9.

Chapter 9 Moving Beyond the Mythology

1. Bruce K. Waltke, *The Book of Proverbs: Chapters 15–31*, New International Commentary on the Old Testament (Eerdmans, 2005), 194.

2. Waltke, *Book of Proverbs*, 204.

3. Waltke, *Book of Proverbs*, 205.

4. Jim Jackson and Lynne Jackson, "Connected Families—About," Connected Families, accessed September 18, 2024, https://connectedfamilies.org/about/.

5. Jackson and Jackson, "Connected Families—About."

6. C. S. Lewis, *The Weight of Glory and Other Addresses* (MacMillan, 1949), 15. *The Weight of Glory* by CS Lewis © copyright 1949 CS Lewis Pte Ltd. Extract used with permission.

MARISSA FRANKS BURT (MTh, Columbia International University) is a novelist, editor, teacher, and cohost of the *At Home with the Lectionary* and *In the Church Library* podcasts. She lives in a small town in Washington's Snoqualmie Valley with her husband, six children, and heaps of books.

KELSEY KRAMER MCGINNIS (PhD, University of Iowa) is a musicologist, educator, and correspondent for *Christianity Today*, writing on worship practices and Christian subculture. She is an adjunct professor at Grand View University in Des Moines and previously worked at the University of Iowa Center for Human Rights.

Connect with Marissa

https://marissaburt.com

@mburtwrites

mburtwrites.bsky.social

Connect with Kelsey

Kelsey Kramer McGinnis

@kelseykmcginnis

@kkramermcginnis

@kelseykmcginnis